D1230920

The Cambridge English Course

LIBR

WITHDRAWN

1 Practice Book

Michael Swan and Catherine Walter

Cambridge University Press

Cambridge

New York   New Rochelle   Melbourne   Sydney

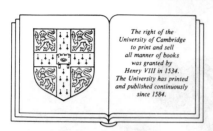

The right of the University of Cambridge to print and sell all manner of books was granted by Henry VIII in 1534. The University has printed and published continuously since 1584.

Published by the Press Syndicate of the University of Cambridge
The Pitt Building, Trumpington Street, Cambridge CB2 1RP
32 East 57th Street, New York, NY10022, USA
10 Stamford Road, Oakleigh, Melbourne 3166, Australia

© Cambridge University Press 1984

First published 1984
Twelfth Printing 1988

Designed by John Youé and Associates, Croydon, Surrey
Typeset by Text Filmsetters Limited, London
Origination by Vyner Litho Plates Limited, London
Printed in Great Britain by Scotprint Ltd, Musselburgh, Scotland

ISBN 0 521 28909 2 Practice Book 1

ISBN 0 521 28908 4 Student's Book 1
Split edition: ISBN 0 521 31028 8 Part A
             ISBN 0 521 31029 6 Part B
             ISBN 0 521 31030 X Part C

ISBN 0 521 28910 6 Teacher's Book 1
ISBN 0 521 27865 1 Test Book 1
ISBN 0 521 24703 9 Cassette Set 1
ISBN 0 521 26223 2 Student's Cassette 1

Copyright
The law allows a reader to make a single copy of part of a book for purposes of private study. It does not allow the copying of entire books or the making of multiple copies of extracts. Written permission for any such copying must always be obtained from the publisher in advance.

Acknowledgements

The authors and publishers are grateful to the following copyright owners for permission to reproduce photographs, illustrations and texts:

page 12: *bl* © British Caledonian Airways.   page 20: *c* Reproduced by permission of The Observer Limited and Guardian Newspapers Limited.   page 26: *r* © 1982 Penguin Books Limited. Reprinted by permission of Penguin Books Limited.   page 29: *t* Reprinted by permission of Oxford & County Newspapers, a division of Westminster Press Limited.   page 31: *br* By Harold Jackson. Reprinted by permission of Guardian Newspapers Limited.   page 34: *br* © André Deutsch.   page 40: *cr* Reprinted by permission of Guardian Newspapers Limited; *b* Reprinted by permission of Johnny Hart and Field Enterprises Incorporated.   page 41: *b* © Statesman & Nation Publishing Company Limited.   page 43: *t* From *This Book is About Schools* by Satu Repo. © Pantheon Books, a division of Random House, Incorporated.   page 51: *c* © 1961 Dover Publications Inc. New York.   page 58: *c* © Guinness Superlatives Limited.   page 59: *r* © John Farquharson Limited, and Walker & Co. New York.   page 64: *t* © Routledge and Kegan Paul Limited and Humanities Press, Inc. (USA).   page 68: *t* Reprinted by permission of London Express News and Feature Services, a division of Express Newspapers Limited.   page 73: *l* © Mirror Group Newspapers Limited.   page 77-8: © Eric Newby.   page 81: *tr* © Associated Newspapers Group plc.   page 83: *b* From *The Joy of Knowledge*, Mitchell Beazley Publishers, London.   page 84: *t* Reprinted by permission of *Autocar* magazine. © Transport Press, a division of Business Press International Limited.   page 87: *b* From *The Royal Canadian Air Force Plan for Physical Fitness*. Reproduced by permission of the Minister of

Supply and Services, Canada; Crown copyright © 1962 by Ottawa, Canada. Reprinted by permission of Simon & Schuster, Inc. Penguin Books Limited, The Government Printing Office, New Zealand.   page 92: *c* Courtesy of British Airways.   page 93: *b* © 1981 King Features Syndicate, Inc. World rights reserved.   page 94: *br* Reproduced by permission of *Punch*.   page 95: *tr* © Pan Books Limited.   page 98: *b* Lyrics of *I Know an Old Lady* by A. Mills/R. Boone are reprinted by permission of Southern Music Publishing Company Limited, Peer International Limited and Peer Muskverlag GmbH.   page 101: *c* Published by The Bodley Head. © Laurence Pollinger Limited and E.P. Dutton & Co., New York.   page 107: *b* © Guinness Superlatives Limited.   page 108: *b* © Piper Books Limited.   page 117: *c* © Churchill Livingstone, Edinburgh.   page 122: *tr* From *Family and School* (Penguin English Project) © Penguin Books Limited; *cr* Reproduced by permission of *Punch*; *b* From *God Bless Love* by Nanette Newman. © The Invalid Children's Aid Association (London) Incorporated.

Colorific Photo Library Limited: p18 *tr*.   Alan Philip: p90.   John Topham Picture Library: p97 *cr*, *cl*.

John Craddock: Suzanne Lihou, Kate Simunek.   David Lewis Management: Bob Harvey.   Linden Artists Limited: Jon Davis, Val Sangster.   Temple Art Agency: Mark Bergin, John James, Mike Whittlesea.   Richard Child, Chris Rawlings, Malcolm Ward, Mike Woodhatch, Youé and Spooner.

(*t* = top   *b* = bottom   *c* = centre   *r* = right   *l* = left)

Contents

Hello

A What's your name?

1 Write the sentences.

1. *What's* your name?

2. Carmen. What's ....?

3. Is .... Joe?

4. No, ... It's ....

5. .... your name Lucy?

6. Yes, it ....

7. Is .... Sally?

8. Yes, ...

9. Hello. .... Anne.

10. ....?

2 Write the full forms.

1. No, it **isn't.** *No, it is not.* ....

2. **What's** your name? ....

3. My **name's** Judy. ....

4. **It's** Mary. ....

3 Write the answers.

1. One + three = *four*

2. Two + two = ...

3. Four + six = ...

4. Seven + one = ...

5. Three + two = ...

6. Five + four = ...

B His name's Robert Redford

1 Put in *my* or *your*.

1. What's .... name?

2. Hello. .... name's Bond – James Bond.

3. 'Is .... name Anne?' 'Yes, that's right.'

4. '........... name's Robert, isn't it?' 'No, it's Mike.'

2 Put in *his* or *her*.

1. .... name's Brigitte.

2. .... name's James.

3. 'Her name's Anne.' 'What's .... surname?'

4. '........... name's Lee.' 'Is that his first name or his surname?'

3 First name or surname?

Anne ...*First name*...........   King ....

Robert ....   Jane ....

Bardot ....   Fonda ....

Bond ....   Jacqueline ....

4 Crossword puzzle.

ACROSS

2. ....'s your name?
3. .... name's Jacqueline Onassis.
6. 'Is .... name Paul?' 'Yes, it is.'
7. Not *her*.
8. Yes, ... is.

(Solution on page 127.)

DOWN

1. What's your ....?
4. Yes, that's ....
5. Not *yes*.
6. Not *no*.

C How are you?

1 Write the answers.

1. 'Hello.' '*Hello*...'

2. 'How are you?' '..........., ...'

3. 'What's your name?' '........... ....'

4. 'How do you do?' '........... ....?'

2 Complete the conversations.

Excuse .... Is .... name Alice Stevens?'

No, ... sorry. .... Alice Carter.'

———◇———

.... me. .... you Bill Wallace?'

..........., I ....'

Hello, Bill. .... name's Jane Marks.'

3 Write the answers.

1. Fourteen + three = ...

2. Nine + four = ...

3. Seventeen − six = ...*eleven*...........................

4. Fifteen − three = ...

5. Eight + eight = ...

6. Twenty − five = ...

5

D Where are you from?

1 Read these words with the correct stress.

Aus**tra**lia	Aus**tra**lian
Germany	**Ger**man
England	**Eng**lish
Britain	**Brit**ish
Italy	I**tal**ian
China	Chi**nese**
Ja**pan**	Japa**nese**

2 Write the full forms.

1. **I'm** English. *I am English.*
2. No, it **isn't.** ....
3. **He's** from Tanzania. ....
4. **She's** American. ....
5. **I'm** from Oxford. ....
6. **Where's** she from? ....

3 Put the adjectives with the right pictures.

Russian	French
Japanese	Cuban
Swiss	British
Egyptian	Chinese
German	Greek

1. *Swiss*............ chocolate

2. a .... dancer

3. an .... pyramid

4. a .... camera

5. a .... statue

6. a .... car

7. a .... car

8. .... perfume

9. a .... cigar

10. a .... plate

Jobs

A What do you do?

1 Put in *I, you, he, she, it, my, your, his* or *her*.

1. 'Are .... Mary Lewis?' 'Yes, ... am.'

2. She's from Spain. .... name's Carmen.

3. ....'s from Japan. His name's Mr Watanabe.

4. 'Are .... Italian?' 'No, I'm Greek.'

5. 'Is your name John Collett?' 'No, ... isn't.'

6. .... name's Alice Stephens. I'm a dentist.

2 Say these words with the correct stress.

artist   Good**bye**
elec**tri**cian   u**ni**ted
engi**neer**   Ex**cuse** me
architect   Chi**nese**
dentist   **Bri**tish
surname   four**teen**
He**llo**

3 Put some more words in these lists.

A		AN
1. *a doctor*	1. *an electrician*
2.	2. ....
3.	3. ....
4.	4. ....
5.	
6.	

4 Fill in the blanks.

A: *What's your name* .... ?
B: It's Smith.
A: .... , Mr Smith?
B: James.
A: .... ?
B: I'm an electrician.

A: .... photographer?
B: No, ... accountant.
A: Oh!

A: .... doctor?
B: No, ... actress.

A: .... pilot?
B: Yes, ...

7

B I'm an actress. And you?

1 Put in *I, you, he, she, am, 'm, are, 're, is* or *'s*.

1. George is Swiss. .... is from Geneva.
2. 'Mrs Alexander isn't English.' 'No? Where's .... from?'
3. 'Are you American?' 'Yes, I ....'
4. 'What do .... do?' '............'m a doctor.'
5. '............ you married?' 'Yes, I ....'
6. 'What'............ your name?' 'Charles.'
7. '............ your name Alice?' 'No, it ....n't.'
8. 'What does Mary do?' '............ .... a shop assistant.'

2 Write the questions.

1. '..?' 'No, I'm single.'
2. '*What do you do*............?' 'I'm a doctor.'
3. '..?' 'Australia.'
4. '..?' 'John Cagney.'
5. '..?' 'No, it's Mary.'

3 Put in the missing words.

1. 'Are you Italian?' 'No, I'm .... France.'
2. I .... a little Portuguese.
3. 'What's your ....?' 'Michael.' 'And your ....?' 'Smith.'
4. Excuse ....
5. '...................... are you?' 'Fine, ...'

C I'm very well, thank you

1 Put in *am, 'm not, are(n't), 's* or *isn't*.

1. Hello. How .... you?
2. How .... your daughter today?
3. 'Are you English?' 'Yes, I ....'
4. 'Judith .... a doctor.' 'No, she .... She's a dentist.'
5. 'Are you married?' 'No, I ....'

2 Morning, afternoon, evening or night?

1. *morning or evening*....
2. ....
3. ....

4. ....
5. ....
6. ....

8

3 Complete the dialogues.

Dialogue 1

A: ....

B: Not bad. And you?

A: ....

Dialogue 2

A: ....

B: Good afternoon, Mr Kowalski. I'm fine, thank you. And you?

A: ....

Dialogue 3

A: Hello. I'm Polly. What's your name?

B: ....

....?

A: No, I'm Australian. And you?

B: ....

.... married?

A: Yes, I am. Oh, dear! It's 10.45! I must go. Bye!

B: ....

D How old are you?

1 Correct these sentences.

1. whats your name

   What's your name?

2. how old are you

   ....

3. im an engineer

   ....

4. suzanne is french

   ....

5. are you an architect

   ....

6. john isnt in england

   ....

7. shes twenty seven

   ....

2 Match words and numbers.

55	five	6	sixty-six	99	ninety
15	fifty-five	16	six	90	nineteen
50	fifty	60	sixteen	19	ninc
5	fifteen	66	sixty	9	ninety-nine

3 Write these numbers in words.

76 *seventy-six*   88 ....

32 ....   17 ....

23 ....   54 ....

14 ....   61 ....

30 ....   12 ....

47 ....

4 Which one is different?

1. morning   evening   night   (name)
2. Hi   How   Where   What
3. Italian   British   Japan   American
4. Hi.   Thanks.   Fine.   Good morning.
5. fine   very well   not bad   good
6. two   twenty-eight   seven   sixteen   six
7. eighty-two   five   thirty   ninety-five   ten

People

A I've got three children

1 Put in *his, her, their, is* or *are*.

1. (Monica) and (her) mother ..are... both doctors.

2. (Philippe) ..is.. French, and (his) wife .... German.

3. Joyce Price .... a photographer, and .... brother .... an accountant.

4. My sister and I .... American, but our grandparents .... Greek.

5. Sonia .... a doctor, and .... mother is a doctor too.

6. Henry's mother .... a shop assistant. .... name is Lucy.

7. George and Karen .... British; .... daughter .... married to an American.

8. Alice and Bill .... doctors, and .... son is a medical student.

9. What .... your brother's name?

10. 'John and Matthew .... brothers.' 'What .... surname?'

2 Pronounce:

John's   Mark's   Joyce's   Ann's
Alan's   Ronald's   Greece's   an artist's
Alice's   Mr Nash's

3 Rewrite the sentences.

1. **Sonia's** a doctor.

....She is a doctor.........................

2. **Sonia's** husband is American.

...Her husband is American..........

3. **Philip's** married to Sonia.

...He is married to Sonia...........

4. **John's** wife is a doctor.

...His wife is a doctor.............

5. **Sally** is George's cousin.

....

6. **Andrew's** an accountant.

....

7. **Karen's** British.

....

8. **Karen's** mother is British.

....

9. **Sonia's** mother and father are doctors.

....

10. **Philip's** Peter's father.

....

4 Draw your family tree. Write five sentences about your family.

....
....
....
....
....
....

B This is Judy

1 Change the sentences.

1. My mother and I are both tall.
   We are both tall.

2. Alex and George are very good-looking.
   They are very good-looking.

3. Susan is an air-hostess.
   She is an air-hostess.

4. My parents and I are fair.

   ....

5. My children are fairly intelligent.

   ....

6. Mary is very slim.

   ....

7. Andrew is not very tall.

   ....

8. Joan and Philip are tall and dark.

   ....

9. Mr and Mrs Carter are American.

   ....

10. John and I are fairly good-looking.

   ....

11. You and your brother both speak German, don't you?

   ....

2 Make questions.

1. your brother | a policeman?
   Is your brother a policeman?

2. his parents | English?
   Are his parents English?

3. they | American?

   ....

4. you and your wife | British?

   ....

5. John and Polly | doctors?

   ....

6. Alison | pretty?

   ....

7. your boyfriend | tall?

   ....

8. your dentist | good-looking?

   ....

9. Ingrid and Christiane | German?

   ....

3 EITHER: write sentences about your family and friends. For example:

My mother is tall and dark. She is very good-looking. My friend Maria is not very tall. She is pretty and very intelligent.

OR: cut pictures out of magazines and write about the people:

She's tall and fair

C An interview

1 Write the answers.

1. Thirty-seven + six = *forty-three*
2. Twenty-eight + four = ...
3. Sixty-nine + seven = ...

4. Eighteen + three = ...
5. Sixty-six + thirty-three = ...
6. Seventy-five + twenty-five = ...

2 Complete the dialogue.

A: Good morning, Mrs Martin.

B: ....

A: Please sit down.

B: ....

A: ....?

B: Thirty-three.

A: ....?

B: Yes, I ....

A: What is ....'s name?

B: Alex.

A: And ....?

B: Thirty-two.

A: Have you got any ....?

B: Yes, ... A boy and a ....
(phone rings)

A: .... me, Mrs Martin. Hello? Yes. Yes.
I'm ...., I .... know. No. Goodbye.
I'm ...., Mrs Martin. Now, you want to borrow some money.

B: Yes.

3 Read this text. Look up the underlined words in a dictionary.

When Ann Bostock joined British Caledonian Airways as a pilot in the summer of 1976, she was their first woman pilot.

Her father and brother took up flying as a hobby, and she got her private pilot's licence after graduating from Oxford. While she studied for her commercial pilot's licence she worked as a flying instructor and then an air-taxi pilot.

12

D What time is it?

1 Try this crossword.

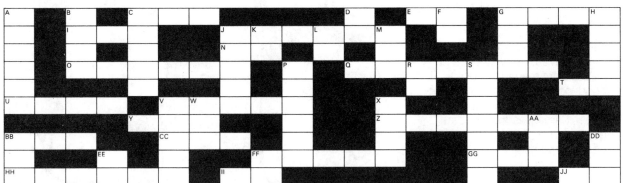

ACROSS

C. 4 + 2.
E. Leonardo da Vinci was a poet, ... artist and an engineer.
G. $3 \times 2 - 1$.
I. $6 - 5 + 4 - 3 - 2 + 1$.
J. *C across* $\times 3 + 2$.
N. 'Is Karsten Danish?' 'Yes, ... is.'
O. 'Are your grandparents Italian?' 'No, ... not.'
Q. 1, 2, 3, 4 etc.
T. What time is ....?
U. Three threes.
V. I've got .... children; two girls and a boy.
Y. My mother's American. ....'s from California.
Z. I speak a little ....
BB. *G across* $\times 2$.
CC. .... you married?
FF. Mother's brother.
GG. No, I'm ....
HH. It's eleven ....
II. What time .... it?
JJ. Good morning, ... Harris.

DOWN

A. 'Where are you from?' '............?' 'Where are you from?'
B. I'm sorry, I .... know.
C. 10 − 3.
D. 'Is your name Bernard?' 'No, ... isn't.'
F. 'Are you married?' '............, I'm not.'
G. *C down* − 3.
H. *G down* $\times 2$.
J. Sonia is Alan and Peter's mother; Philip is .... father.
K. 'Are you Mr and Mrs Harris?' 'Yes, ... are.'
L. The same as *F down*.
M. Thank ....
P. 6 + 5.
R. Good morning. .... name is Henry Martin.
S. Alice is English. She's from ....
V. 'Sit down, please.' '............ you.'
W. She's tall, but .... husband is very short.
X. We are.
AA. .... down, please.
BB. ...., 4, 6, 8, 10.
DD. Mary and .... sister are very pretty.
EE. How do you ....?
FF. United States.

(Solution on page 127.)

2 Change the sentences as in the example.
Example:

Joyce has got a son. He is fourteen.

Joyce's son is fourteen

1. Peter has got a sister. She is very pretty.

....

2. My mother has got a brother. He is a doctor.

....

3. Anne has got a boyfriend. He is tall and good-looking.

....

4. Robert has got a girlfriend. She is not very pretty.

....

5. Mrs Lewis has got children. They are both students.

....

3 Read this with a dictionary.

Judy Parker is twenty-two. She is a medical student. Judy is intelligent and very pretty, with a good sense of humour. She is a nice woman. Her boyfriend's name is Sam Watson. Sam is twenty-seven. He works in a bank as assistant manager. He is good-looking, but he is not a very nice man. Judy loves Sam very much. Sam loves money, cars, good food, whisky, travel and beautiful women.

It's a long story
PART I

Places

A Glasgow is an industrial city…

 1 Make some sentences like these.

Rouen is a large town in France.
Marrakesh is a city in Morocco.
Barnstaple is a small town in the south-west of England
Seville and Jerez are towns in the south of Spain.

2 Think of *five* places in your country. Write them in the correct places in this table.

	north	south	east	west
small village				
small town				
town				
large town				
city				
large city				

14

3 Fill in the blanks.

Houston, Beaumont and Galveston .... in the
south-east .... Texas. Houston and Beaumont
.... industrial cities; Houston is ....
large. Galveston is a tourist .... near Houston.
Dallas .... Amarillo are in the ....
Dallas is a large .... city in the north-east,
.... Amarillo is a .... town in the
north-west, ... New Mexico. Panhandle is
.... small town near Amarillo.

a
and
and
are
are
of
very
small
near
centre
north
industrial

4 *a or the?*

1. Nice is on ..*the*.... south coast of France.
2. Brindisi is .... small town in .... south of Italy.
3. Budapest is .... capital city of Hungary.
4. Vienna is .... tourist centre.

5. Shari is in .... north of Japan.
6. Thessalonica is .... large city in Greece.
7. Athens is .... capital city of Greece.
8. Campos is on .... east coast of Brazil.

B Where's that?

1 Write out the full forms.

1. Who's that? ..*Who is*..........
2. We're French. ....
3. Where's your mother from? ....
4. That's in Brazil. ....
5. He's good-looking! ....
6. I'm in New York. ....
7. They aren't on the beach. ....

2 Circle the word that is different.

1. Brazil Japan China (Acapulco)
2. north east coast west
3. industrial centre large central
4. mother wife daughter woman
5. small town village city
6. We're Who's What's Where's

3 Fill in the blanks.

1. .... ?
.................................?
No, I'm from Portugal.
I'm from Peru. And you?
My wife's from San Juan.
No, it's in Puerto Rico.
Where's your mother from?
2. ....
....
4. ....
.................................?

15

C Where's Stockholm?

1 Yes or no? Find the answers in an atlas. Correct the sentences if they are not right.

1. Italy is south of Switzerland.
   .....*Yes*.....

2. Brazil is east of Peru.

   ....

3. The capital of Niger is Lagos.
   No. The capital of Niger is Niamey.

4. Casablanca is a city in the north of Algeria.

   ....

5. Vienna is in the north-east of Austria.

   ....

6. New York is the capital of the USA.

   ....

7. Moscow is in the east of the USSR.

   ....

8. Hungary is north-east of Rumania.

   ....

9. Rio de Janeiro is the capital of Brazil.

   ....

10. Barcelona is in the south of Spain.

   ....

2 Reading for information. Read the three texts and find the answers to these questions. How quickly can you finish? Use a dictionary if necessary.

1. What is the population of Nairobi? ....
2. True or false? The population of Albania is 30% Moslem. ....
3. Do Guatemalans speak Spanish? ....
4. Is Kenya in West Africa? ....
5. Where is Tiquisate? ....
6. Where is Tirana? ....
7. Who speaks Luo? ....
8. The quetzal is the currency of ....
9. What is the area of Guatemala? ....
10. Where is Shkodër? ....
11. What is the population of Albania? ....
12. True or false? Yugoslavia is south-west of Albania. ....
13. True or false? Mexico is north of Guatemala.

   ....
14. What is the capital of Guatemala?

   ....

ALBANIA
Area: 11,100 sq. mi. (28,416 sq. km.). *Population:* 2,500,000. *Official name:* People's Socialist Republic of Albania. *Capital:* Tirana. *Nationality:* Albanian. *Languages:* Gheg, Tosk, Greek. *Religion:* 50% Moslem, 20% Orthodox, 10% Roman Catholic. *Currency:* Lek. *Location:* South-east Europe, on the west coast of the Balkan peninsula. Albania is bordered on the north and east by Yugoslavia, on the south by Greece, and on the west by the Adriatic. *Largest cities:* Tirana 170,000, Durrës 80,000, Vlorë 57,000, Korcë 53,000, Shkodër 49,000.

GUATEMALA
Area: 42,042 sq. mi. (107,628 sq. km.). *Population:* 6,000,000. *Official name:* Republic of Guatemala. *Capital:* Guatemala. *Nationality:* Guatemalan. *Languages:* Spanish, Maya-Quiché. *Religion:* Roman Catholic. *Currency:* Quetzal. *Location:* Central America. Guatemala is bordered on the north by Mexico, on the east by Belize and the Caribbean, on the south-east by Honduras and El Salvador, on the south-west by the Pacific Ocean, and on the west by Mexico. *Largest cities* (1973 census): Guatemala 700,538, Tiquisate 67,555, Quezaltenango 65,526, Escuintla 64,851.

KENYA
Area: 224,960 sq. mi. (575,898 sq. km.). *Population:* 13,900,000 (1977 est.). *Official name:* Republic of Kenya. *Capital:* Nairobi. *Nationality:* Kenyan. *Languages:* Swahili, English, Kikuyu, Luo, and many others. *Religion:* 40% animist, 50% Christian, 6% Moslem or Hindu. *Currency:* Kenya shilling. *Location:* East Africa. Kenya is bordered

on the north by Sudan and Ethiopia, on the east by Somalia and the Indian Ocean, on the south by Tanzania, and on the west by Uganda. *Largest cities:* Nairobi 750,000, Mombasa 334,000, Nakuru 50,000, Kisumu 35,000.

3 Write a similar text about your country, on another piece of paper.

D It's an exciting place

1 *and* or not? Examples:

Vézelay is a nice ....—........ quiet village.

Vézelay is nice *..and..* quiet.

1. Bilbao is a large .... industrial town.

2. Osaka is noisy .... exciting.

3. John is a tall .... good-looking man.

4. Burford is a pretty .... English town.

5. My mother is a short .... dark woman.

6. I am tall .... dark, but my brother is tall .... fair.

2 Write these numbers in words.

342 *three hundred and forty-two*

768 ....

1,943 ....

22 ....

1,000,000 ....

110 ....

75,000 ....

999 ....

4,187 ....

81 ....

40 ....

3 Think of five cities, towns or villages in your country. Put their names in this table.

	town	city	village
quiet			
noisy			
pretty			
polluted			
exciting			

It's a long story PART 2

4 Read this with a dictionary.

Judy is worried. She doesn't know where Sam is. The bank manager doesn't know where Sam is, either. He is very worried.

Sam is in Brazil, in a small town on the coast near Rio de Janeiro, with £50,000 of the bank's money. He is sitting in a bar near the beach, drinking a large martini and writing a letter to Judy.

17

Home

A A house

1

Jenny lives in a small flat and Sally lives in a big flat. Here is some information about the two flats.

Jenny's flat

two rooms:
living room   very small kitchen
and:
small bathroom with a shower and a toilet
in the kitchen:
small fridge
in the living room:
black and white TV

Sally's flat

four rooms:
living room   two bedrooms   big kitchen
and:
bathroom   separate toilet
in the kitchen:
big fridge   dishwasher
in the living room:
colour TV

Write about Sally's flat by completing the following description.

There .... four .... in Sally's flat: a living room, two .... and a big

.... is .... bathroom too, and a separate .... In

the kitchen .... a big .... and a dishwasher. ....

.... colour .... in the ....

Now write about Jenny's flat.

2 Write about the house or flat of someone you know (your mother/brother/friend/...).

3 Believe it or not.

There is a river in France called 'Aa', and a village in France named 'Y'. In Sweden, there is a town called 'Å'. In Wales, there is a small village called 'Llanfairpwllgwyngyllgogerychwyrndrobwll-llantisiliogogogoch'.

There are only twelve letters in the Hawaiian alphabet: A, E, H, I, K, L, M, N, O, P, U and W.

There is a street in Canada that is 1,900km long.

There are about 790,000 words in English.

There are about 5,000 languages in the world (845 in India).

There are six different languages in Great Britain and Ireland (English, Welsh, Scots Gaelic, Irish Gaelic, Manx and Cornish).

When the time in Moscow is 2 p.m., it is midnight in Anadyr, on the other side of the Soviet Union.

B Where do you live?

1 Put in the correct preposition (*at, in* or *on*).

1. I live .... 14 St Andrew's Place, Dundee.

2. My father lives .... a small house ....
North London.

3. My girlfriend's flat is .... the seventh
floor.

4. Do you live .... a house or a flat?

5. 'Where's the toilet, please?' '........... the
second floor.'

6. 'Is there a doctor near here?' 'Yes, ... 37
High Street.'

7. I lived .... America from 1976 to 1978.

8. She lives .... Pentonville Road.

2 *Live* or *lives*?

1. My Aunt Sally .... in New Jersey.

2. Where do you ....?

3. We .... at 141 Riverside Avenue, Cardiff.

4. My brother's wife .... in Chicago.

5. The Prime Minister .... at 10 Downing
Street.

3 Say the names of these letters.

A   E   I   H   Y   R   K   W   G   Q   V   J   X   Z   U

Spell these words aloud.

north   name   time   five   nine   geography   east
tall   intelligent   friend   nice   girl   Japan   John

Say these abbreviations.

USSR   TWA   BBC   EEC   USA   OK

4 Match the times.

9.45	a quarter past eleven
6.30	half past eight
7.20	twenty-five past three
11.15	twenty to eleven
3.25	a quarter to ten
5.45	half past six
8.30	twenty past seven
10.40	a quarter past six
6.15	a quarter to six

C What's your phone number?

1 Complete these dialogues.

Dialogue 1

A: Hello.

B: Is .... Brighton 61664?

A: No, ... is Brighton 61554.

B: Oh, I'm .... number. Goodbye.

A: ....

Dialogue 2

A: Warwick 39522.

B: Hello. .... I speak .... Robert?

A: One .... I'm sorry. ....'s not
.... Can I take a ....?

B: Yes. Please tell him that John called.

A: ....

B: .... very much. ....

A: ....

2 Read this with a dictionary.

telephone

British **TELECOM** **Pay-on-Answer**

Have money ready 5p 10p

Minimum fee – 5p

1 Lift handset
Listen for dial tone –

(Continuous purring

~~~~~~~~~~~~~~~~~~~~~

or high-pitched hum).

2 Dial number
Listen for ringing tone* –
(in the UK a brr-brr)

᷉᷉ ᷉᷉

*Varies according to country being dialled

When dialled number answers –
Listen for paytone –
(rapid pips)

• • • • • • • • • • • • • • • • • • •

3 Press in money
Speak when connected

To continue a dialled call – when you hear paytone (rapid pips) again, or anytime during call, press in more money.

4 Replace handset

(Reproduced by permission of British Telecommunications.)

3 Read *five* of these advertisements with a dictionary.

HAMPSTEAD VILLAGE. Standing on a prominent corner position. A spacious 1st flr. flat in good order. Lge. living rm. 2 dble beds. kit. bath & w.c. c.h. £49,950 Sole Agents. ANSCOMBE & RINGLAND 115 7941.

DULWICH. Town house. 4 bedrooms (3 double), lounge/dining room, kitchen and bathroom, 2nd WC, utility area, garden, garage. Victoria 12 mins. Gas central heating. Near amenities. £46,000 ono. Freehold. 958 0670. View Sunday.

HERNE HILL, SE24. Pretty garden flat, 2 rooms, k & b. £23,500. 274 9737.

FULHAM. Flat, 3 rooms, k & b. £21,250. 01-950 6668.

WESTMINSTER, SW1. Delightful 1 bed flat in newly modernised block. Lge hall, recep/dining/new fully fitted kit, new bath, incl CH. Lift. New lease. A snip at £42,500. Sole agents. LEAVERS 01-126 1629. Ref. DB1/Res.

LAKE DISTRICT NATLAND, NEAR KENDAL
Well built modern detached bungalow. 3 bedrooms, kitchen, bathroom, separate w.c., lounge/dining room. Gas central heating. Garage. Small garden with greenhouse.
£28,000
Telephone 63 096 2008

PUTNEY HEATH, SW15. A selection of 4 and 3 bedroom flats in a most attractive block directly overlooking the Heath. All flats have constant hot water and central heating and have accommodation comprising 3 bedrooms, 2 reception rooms and bathroom or 4 bedrooms, 2 reception rooms and 2 bathrooms.
Long Leasehold. Prices between £50,000 and £100,000.

ST MARGARETS/TWICKENHAM. 3 bedroomed terrace family home. CH, large garden, garage. £32,200. Tel. 01-732 8926.

ELVASTON PLACE, SW7. Studio room, kitchen & bathroom & dressing room. 98 yr lease. £29,000. 365 1828. COOTES.

ELVASTON PLACE, SW7. Bedroom, reception, bathroom, separate shower room, kitchen. 99 yr lease. £39,000. 365 8281. COOTES.

HIGHGATE AREA, just off Hornsey Lane. A Victorian terraced house, tastefully modernised with 4 bedrooms, bathroom/WC, grd flr cloakroom, double reception, large kitchen/breakfast room, cellar, gas CH, garden. Freehold, £59,950. EDMUND CUDE & BOOTH ESTATE AGENTS. 01-340 50

REGENTS PARK, NW1. 2nd fl flat at present 5 rms, k&b. Could be 3 large rms, k&b. Lse 99 years. £47,000. PHILIP FISHER & CO. 01-779 7229.

BLOOMSBURY, WC1. 5th fl flat in popular block. Lift. Excellent condn. 3 beds, 2 recps, k&b. Lse 97 yrs. £42,500. PHILIP FISHER & CO. 01-726 7792.

FULHAM, SW6. Well modernised corner house, 4 beds, 2 baths, double recep, kitchen, cellar, walled garden. Nr Parsons Green. Must sell. Bargain £69,950 (01) 574 9731.

WALES

AN IDEAL HOME – BEST POSITION IN LLANDUDNO
Four bedrooms, lounge, dining-room, dining/kitchen, large sun lounge, full central heating. Double glazing, many fitted carpets and extras.
Price: £55,000
For particulars tel:
0483 92435

ALBERT BRIDGE ROAD, SW11. A selection of 2/4 bedroom flats. Well modernised with super views over Battersea Park, Long leases. Prices: £45,000-£59,950.

ST JOHN'S WOOD, Hamilton Terrace. Delightful mod flat, 2 bdroms, rec, k&b, gge, CH, ultra mod, 55 yrs. £44,500. CROUCH & LEES. Open Sun. 11-1 p.m.

NEW KINGS ROAD, SW6. Ground floor garden flat. Large reception room, 2 bedrooms, kitchen/diner, bathroom. Needs loving decoration, 99 year lease. £29,500. FULHAM & CHELSEA ESTATES. 01-300 8134/5.

CLAPHAM COMMON. Totally modernised 5 bedroom, 2 bathroom house. Bargain at £52,500 for quick sale 01-766 7209.

THE HOME MARKET
106 Dawes Road SW6
01-389 3818
THE NO COMMISSION
PROPERTY SHOP

STOCKWELL SW8. Completely modernised 3 bed, 2 recep, 2 bath, house Gas CH. Freehold £36,000.

4 What do you think these abbreviations mean?

(first advertisement)

1st flr ....

Lge ....

rm ....

dble ....

kit ....

(third advertisement)

k & b ....

D More than one

1 Try the crossword puzzle.

ACROSS

3. There's a big .... in my flat.
5. Where .... you live?
6. Excuse me. ....'s the toilet?
9. 1st.
11. Her .... is in Manchester.
13. My wife and I live in Edinburgh. .... phone number is 314 6829.
14. What's .... phone number?
17. ....'s the time?
18. The Prime Minister lives .... 10 Downing Street.
20. 'Are you American?' '............, I'm not.'
21. The American first floor is the British .... floor.

4. It's 8 o'clock in London. What .... is it in Moscow?
7. My sister's an architect. .... name's Lucy.
8. Jane and Philip are tall and fair, but .... mother and father are short and dark.
9. My flat's on the fourth ....
10. My brother and his wife are doctors. .... live in London.
12. Helen is my mother. Helen is Philip's mother. So Philip is my ....
15. There's a beautiful girl in the flat .... the second floor.
16. The same as 18 across.
18. The United Kingdom consists of England, Scotland, Wales .... Northern Ireland.
19. It's 60 miles from Oxford .... London.

(Solution on page 127.)

DOWN

1. .... are 50 States in the USA.
2. 'Where's Mary?' '............ the living room.'
3. 'Where's the station?' 'I'm sorry, I don't ....'

2 Match the words and the numbers.

505	five thousand and fifty
5,005	five thousand and fifteen
5,015	five thousand, one hundred and fifty
5,050	five hundred and five
515	five thousand, five hundred
5,500	five hundred and fifteen
5,150	five thousand and five

3 Read this with a dictionary.

It's a long story PART 3

Rio, Tuesday.

Darling Judy,
       Well here I am in Brazil. It's very warm here, and the sea is nice for swimming. The women here are very beautiful, and very, very friendly. But I miss you, Judy. Please come and stay with me in Brazil. Can you take the 13·25 flight from London to Rio on April 14th? I'll meet you at the airport.
All my love
Sam

Unit 6

Habits

A What do you like?

1 Fill in the blanks.

1. '....................... Mozart?' 'No, I
   ....'

2. 'I .... beer, but I ....
   whisky at all.' 'Don't you?'

3. 'I like Picasso very much. .... you?'
   'Yes, I ....'

4. What sort of books .... you
   ....?

5. Everybody .... Sally.
   Nobody .... Ann.

6. Only two people in my family ....
   dancing.

2 Put in *he*, *she*, *him* or *her*.

1. John's nice. I like .... a lot.

2. 'Is Mary at home?' 'Yes, ... is.' 'Can I
   speak to ...., please?' 'Of course.'

3. 'That's my mother over there.' '...........'s very
   pretty.'

4. Ann likes Bill, but he doesn't like .... much.

5. 'My brother's a shop assistant.' 'Where
   does .... work?'

6. 'What do you think of Peter?' 'I quite like
   ....'

3

Four people work in an office: two women and two
   men.
Anne likes Catherine, but she dislikes the two men.
Peter doesn't like the person that Anne likes, but
   he likes Anne.
Only one person likes Catherine.
John likes two people.
One person doesn't like Anne. Who is it?

(Solution on page 127.)

4 Write a poem about your likes and dislikes.
Use a dictionary if you want to. Example:

I quite like the sea.
I like my friends and my family.
I love the sun, strawberries, dancing and cats.
I don't like fast cars or snails.
I hate violence.

B Work

1 Write *do* or *does* in each blank.

1. .... your father work in a garage?

2. What time .... you finish work in the evening?

3. What .... your husband do?

4. .... both your children go to the same school?

5. Where .... they have lunch?

6. .... your grandmother work?

7. When .... Andrew's sister have lunch?

22

2 Choose the correct verb for each blank.

1. Mechanics usually .... work at eight o'clock.

2. In Spain, people ....dinner at ten o'clock in the evening.

3. My cousin Tom .... in Germany.

4. The village shop .... at nine o'clock in the morning.

5. Anita .... children's clothes and shoes.

6. I .... cereal and milk for breakfast.

7. Brian .... old clocks.

VERBS

have/has
live/lives
open/opens
repair/repairs
sell/sells
start/starts

3 Make eight sentences.

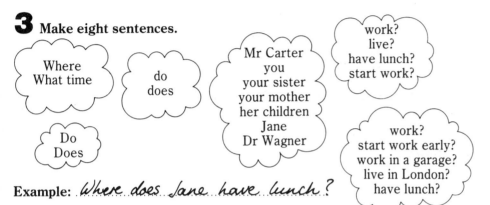

Where
What time

do
does

Mr Carter
you
your sister
your mother
her children
Jane
Dr Wagner

work?
live?
have lunch?
start work?

Do
Does

work?
start work early?
work in a garage?
live in London?
have lunch?

Example: *Where does Jane have lunch?*

4 Read the texts. *Don't* use a dictionary. What jobs do you think the six people have? **Possibilities:** electrician, secretary, doctor, dentist, air hostess, photographer, bank manager, bus driver, artist, lorry driver, singer.

A. She speaks four languages. She works very long hours, but she does not work every day. She likes people and travel, and she travels a lot in her work.

Answer: *She is an* ....

B. She doesn't work in an office. She works very long hours, and she often gets up at night – it's a tiring job. She likes people. She does not speak any foreign languages. She loves her job.

Answer: ....

C. He gets up at half past seven every day, has breakfast at eight o'clock, and starts work at half past nine. He works in an office; he has two secretaries and two telephones. He does not work on Saturdays. He likes people and mathematics.

Answer: ....

D. He usually gets up at eleven o'clock, and has breakfast at lunchtime. He works at home. He works in the afternoons, but not every day. Sometimes he works very long hours; sometimes he does not work at all. He loves his job.

Answer: ....

E. She lives in a big city. She gets up at two o'clock in the afternoon, and has breakfast at three o'clock. She works from 9 p.m. until 2 a.m. She goes to and from work by taxi. She does not like her job much, and she does not like the people where she works.

Answer: ....

F. He gets up at two o'clock in the morning. He has breakfast and lunch in motorway restaurants. He works sitting down, and he travels a lot in his work. He likes his job.

Answer: ....

C What newspaper do you read?

1 Write the full forms.

aren't *are not*

haven't ....

doesn't ....

don't ....

I'm ....

we're ....

you're ....

they're ....

2 Answer *Yes, I do; No, I don't; Yes, I am;* or *No, I'm not.*

1. Are you tall? ....

2. Do you like cats? ....

3. Are you married? ....

4. Are you American? ....

5. Do you speak French? ....

6. Do you work on Saturdays? ....

7. Are you a student? ....

8. Do you like your work? ....

9. Do you like children? ....

3 *It, them, him* or *her?* Change the sentences. Use your dictionary.

1. I like bananas. *I like them.*

2. I hate whisky. ....

3. Alice loves children. ....

4. Children love Alice. ....

5. I don't like rock music. ....

6. Can I speak to Bill, please? ....

7. Do you like work? ....

8. She loves fast cars. ....

9. I don't like Mrs Harris very much. ....

10. I hate rain. ....

11. You can't speak to John. He isn't here. ....

12. Do you like big dogs? ....

4 Make at least ten sentences from this table. Use *neither, both* and *but.*

NAME	PLAYS FOOTBALL	LIKES BEER	READS NOVELS	IS INTERESTED IN POLITICS	GOES TO CHURCH	GOES CAMPING
Robert	No	Yes	No	Yes	No	Yes
Janet	Yes	No	Yes	No	Yes	No
Kevin	Yes	Yes	Yes	No	No	No
Philip	Yes	Yes	No	No	No	Yes
Sue	No	Yes	No	Yes	Yes	Yes

Examples: *Robert neither plays football nor reads novels.*
Neither Robert nor Sue plays football.
Janet and Kevin both read novels.
Sue goes to church, but Philip doesn't.

D What does Lorna drink?

1 Give the third-person singular forms of these verbs.

work .....*works*..................... like .... watch ....

get .... go .... finish ....

have .... sell .... study ....

2 Imagine how one of these people spends his/her day, and write about it.

3 Read this with a dictionary.

It's a long story PART 4

Judy is at home. (She lives in a small flat near the bank. It's not very nice.) She's in the living room, drinking a cup of coffee and thinking. Judy's very worried, because she doesn't know what to do. She loves Sam, and she doesn't want to tell the police where he is. But she doesn't want to go to Rio, either. She wants a quiet life.

Judy goes to the window and looks out. There's a police car in the street. Two big policemen are walking towards her house.

Food and drink

 How many calories?

1 Put in *I, you, he, she, we, they, my, your, his, her, our* or *their.*

1. We live in London. .... address is 17 Fox Terrace, Hampstead.

2. 'Where does your sister work?' '............. works in Sheffield.'

3. Susie and Ingrid are German – .... are from Düsseldorf. .... father is a bank manager.

4. My mother lives with .... second husband in Edinburgh.

5. My wife and I are architects. .... work in an office in the centre of Cambridge.

6. 'There's Mr Parslow.' 'What's .... first name?' 'Sam.'

2 Reading for information.
For dinner, you have:
prawns (112g)
two pork chops and a baked potato
fresh raspberries (226g)
How many calories?
Answer: ....

Food	Portion	Calories	Fibre
Plaice, fillets, fried in crumbs	6oz (170g) raw weight	435	1.0
Plums Victoria, dessert	2½oz (70g), average-sized fruit	15	1.5
cooking, stewed without sugar, weighed with stones	6oz (170g)	40	3.5
Pork chop, grilled	7oz (200g) raw weight, fat cut off after grilling	315	0
leg, roast	3oz (85g), lean only	155	0
Pork sausages, grilled	2oz (56g), large sausage, raw weight	135	0
	1oz (28g), 1 chipolata, raw weight	65	0
Porridge	1 oz (28g) oatmeal or porridge oats made up with water	110	2.0
Potato baked	7oz (200g), eaten with skin		
roast	2oz (56g)	170	5.0
instant, mashed	1oz (28g) dry weight	90	1.0
old, boiled and mashed	4oz (113g)	90	4.5
new boiled		90	1.0
canned	4oz (113g)	85	2.5
Prawns, shelled	4oz (113g) drained weight	60	3.0
Prunes, dried with stones	2oz (56g)	60	0
stewed without sugar	1oz (28g), four to five prunes		
Puffed wheat	4oz (113g) cooked weight	20	2.0
Rabbit, stewed	¾oz (21g), average breakfast bowl	85	8.5
Radishes, raw	6oz (170g), weighed on the bone	70	3.5
Raisins	1oz (28g), salad serving	150	0
Raspberries raw	½oz (14g), serving with cereal etc.	5	0.5
canned in syrup	4oz (113g)	35	1.0
Redcurrants, stewed without sugar	4oz (113g), fruit and syrup	30	8.5
	4oz (113g)	95	5.5
		20	8.0

(from *The F-Plan Calorie and Fibre Chart* by Audrey Eyton)

3 Say the plurals of these words, and group them according to the pronunciations of -(e)s.

/z/	/s/	/ɪz/
doors	aunts	messages
doctors	....	....
....	....	....
....	....	....
....	....	....
....	....	

door	message
doctor	night
aunt	match
lamp	tourist
potato	girl
age	morning
race	bed
Italian	orange

4 *Do or does?*

1. Where .... your parents live?
2. What time .... you start work?
3. .... your mother like cooking?
4. .... you like your job?
5. How .... you travel to work?
6. What sort of books .... Mary read?
7. What languages .... Mr Andrews speak?
8. What newspaper .... you read?

B It's terrible

1 With or without *a*?
Match the words and the pictures.

potato
a potato
paper
a paper
glass
a glass
hair
a hair
lamb
a lamb

1. .... 2. .... 3. .... 4. .... 5. ....

6. .... 7. .... 8. .... 9. .... 10. ....

2 Give the prices of some things. Example: *Oranges are 75 cents a kilo.*

3 Write negative answers.

1. 'Are you Spanish?' '.................................'
2. 'Do you know what time it is?' '.................................'
3. 'Is he married?' '.................................'
4. 'Does Mary live with her parents?' '.................................'
5. 'Are we in London?' '.................................'
6. 'Am I speaking to Mrs Collins?' '.................................'
7. 'Do they drink beer?' '.................................'
8. 'Does he speak Chinese?' '.................................'
9. 'Are they married?' '.................................'

Use:

No, I'm not.
No, you aren't.
No, he/she isn't.
No, we aren't.
No, they aren't.

No, I don't.
No, you don't.
No, he/she doesn't.
No, we don't.
No, they don't.

4 Reading for information.
Read the advertisements.

How much will it cost to buy all of these:
a girl's bicycle, a winter coat, 12 lbs (pounds) of apples, two Alsatian puppies (baby dogs), a Renault 12 TL, a violin and three ducks?
Total cost: ....

PARROTS

African Greys
Amazons
Cockatoos
and Macaws

Telephone
**High Wycombe
81714**

CLIPPING AND Trimming, reasonable rates, reliable service. – Tel. Thame 613, evenings/weekends.

CLIPPING, reasonable rates. – Tel. Shipton-under-Wychwood 30599.

DOUBLE HORSE Trailer, twin wooden construction, excellent condition, £750. – Tel. Freeland 81513.

DUCKS, Khaki Campbell and Aylesbury, £1.75 each. – Tel. Cholsey 52035.

RENAULT 30TS hatchback, P reg. approx 41,000 miles hrw, central door locking, electric windows, radio cassette, good condition, 2 months tax and 8 months' MoT, £995. – Tel. Kidlington 031.

... mileage, 1 year's MoT, £650. – Tel. Oxford 26213.

VAUXHALL VIVA, 1967; MoT and taxed, excellent condition for year, undersealed: £155. – Tel. Witney 206.

VW GOLF, 1600 LS, three door P reg, taxed end of April, 50,000 miles approx, needs some attention.£1,500. – Tel. Oxford 21224 after 6.30 pm.

WIRE HAIRED Fox Terrier, champion bred bitch, 6 months, £50. – Cropredy 76.

YORKY DOG, cheap to good home, lovable silky black dog, 4 months old free to good home, Alsatian puppies, £45 each. – For details tel. Fritwell 84.

M & S Winter Coat, classic style, navy, size 14, long, only worn once, as new. £20. – Tel. Oxford 4243, evenings.

GENT'S 3 speed 21" frame, in good condition, complete with lights and pump, £48 ono. – Tel. Oxford 81005.

GIRL'S Raleigh "Flyer" Cycle, suit age approx 7 years, bell, rear basket etc, superb condition, outgrown, £40 ono – Call 47 Ramsons Way (off Daisybank, Radley Road), Abdon, after 3.30 pm.

CASIOTONE 1,000 P Electronic Organ with extras, £300. – Tel. Bicester 140, evenings.

KIMBALL Electric Organ, as new, memory box, rhythms and other features, offers around £450. – Tel. Oxford 27596.

OBOE, wooden Buisson, £375, in excellent condition. – Tel. Henley-on-Thames 624

USED CYCL
Reconditioned and DI
1,000 CYCLES IN STOC
DENTON'
294 Banbury Road
Tel. Oxford 3859

PIANO, satin mahogany u excellent condition. – Tel. Princes Risboroug

UPRIGHT PIANO, regular ed, £160. – Tel. 0543 (weekends), Oxford (weekdays).

UPRIGHT PIANO by Boyd Lt don, in excellent con complete with stool, £2 – Tel. Oxford 86351 afte

VIOLIN, ¾ size with case an £125. – Tel. Oxford 1167

YAMAHA electric Org keyboards, octave bas als, rhythm section, exc condition, £450. – Tel. pton 71.

APPLES, Bramleys, good ke 12 lbs for £1. – Tel. Fre 81731.

BURMESE SEAL Kittens, and females, inoculated registered, ready now. Banbury 11655.

BURMESE KITTENS, fully in lated, very reasonable t ceptional homes. – Tel. O 5084.

C Have you got a good memory?

1 Countable or uncountable?

butter   wool ☐   sheep ☐   beer ☐   rain ☐   bread ☐   banana ☐

£5 note *C*   tomato ☐   bank ☐   music ☐   wine ☐   money ☐

2 Some or any?

1. There is .... beer in the fridge.

2. Are there .... grapes in the kitchen?

3. I've got .... nice friends.

4. Alice hasn't got .... children.

5. Have you got .... American friends?

6. There isn't .... wine in my glass.

7. There aren't .... penguins in Scotland.

8. Has your father got .... brothers and sisters

9. I know .... nice people in Canada.

10. We had .... rain this evening.

3 What food and drink is there in your fridge/kitchen/flat/house? Use *some* and *any*.
Example: *There's some beer in my fridge, but there aren't any tomatoes.*

4 Put in the correct form of the verb.

1. What languages ...*do*.... you *speak*? (speak)

2. They ...*do*... ...*not*... ...*know*... my address. (not know)

3. Where .... your mother ....? (live)

4. What time .... you .... work? (start)

5. Lucy .... on Friday afternoons. (not work)

6. .... Cathy .... reading? (like)

7. .... they ....German in Switzerland? (speak)

8. I watch football, but I .... it. (not play)

9. Robert .... dancing and tennis. (like)

10. Alexandra .... the violin very well. (play)

D Not enough money

1 Put in *how much* or *how many*.

1. .... brothers and sisters have you got?

2. '............ .... English do you speak?' 'Not much.'

3. .... people are there in your family?

4. .... calories are there in a pint of beer?

5. '............ .... money have you got on you?' 'About £5.'

6. .... cheese is there in the fridge?

7. .... languages do you speak?

8. .... children have you got?

2 Make sentences.

I haven't got
I've got

enough   a lot of
too much   too many

money.
work. free time.
friends. clothes.
....

3 Pronounce these words with the correct stress.

tomato   orange   weekend
water   memory   newspaper
banana   travelling   interested
intelligent   depends   language
terrible   everybody   holiday
supermarket   breakfast

4 How many triangles are there?

Answer: ....
(Answer on page 127.)

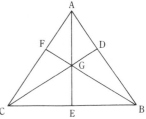

5 Read this with a dictionary.

Hello – is that Croxton 43122? Dr Wagner? Listen, Dr Wagner, this is Judy…Yes, Judy Parker. Listen, I'm in very bad trouble. Can you help?…Trouble with Sam and the bank and the police. I haven't got time to explain…Yes, OK. Please come to my house *at once* with your car. As fast as you can – it's really urgent…23 Carlton Road. Turn right at the station and it's the second street on your left. *Please* hurry! Oh, and come to the *back* door.

It's a long story PART 5

Where?

A Where's the nearest post office?

1 Complete these dialogues.

A: .... ?

B: Over there by the stairs.

A: ....

———◇———

A: Excuse me. Where's Room 8, please?

B: ....

A: ....

———◇———

A: Excuse me. Where's the nearest ....?

B: ....

A: ....

2 Answer these questions. Use *Yes, there is/are, No, there isn't/aren't* or *I don't know.*

1. Is there a bank in your street? ....

2. Is there a swimming pool near your home? ....

3. Is there an armchair in your bedroom? ....

4. Is there a television in your living room? ....

5. Is there a bus stop in your street? ....

6. Are there tigers in Canada? ....

7. Are there elephants in Thailand? ....

8. Are there penguins in Brazil? ....

9. Are there camels in India? ....

10. Is there a cat in your home? ....

3 True or false?

1. The USSR is 31 miles (50km) from the USA. ....

2. In 1710, there were 350 Europeans living in North America. ....

3. The population of Mexico City is 2 million. ....

4. Mont Blanc is 6,000 metres high. ....

5. There are 20 pence (20p) in a pound sterling. ....

6. There are 100 cents (100¢) in a US dollar ($1). ....

7. Edinburgh is in the north of England. ....

8. There are three kilometres in a mile. ....

9. The President of the United States lives in the White House. ....

10. There are penguins in the Arctic. ....

(Answers on page 127.)

4 Make questions. Use *Is/Are there...?*

1. lions | Uganda? *Are there lions in Uganda?*

2. an armchair | your bathroom? ....

3. a hotel | your street? ....

4. a bank | the station? ....

5. camels | Argentina? ....

6. a bus stop | this street? ....

7. a fridge | your kitchen? ....

8. crocodiles | Texas? ....

B   First on the right, second on the left

1 You are in the street near your home, *or* at the town centre in your home town. Answer these questions.

1. Excuse me. Where's the nearest bus stop, please? ....

....

2. Excuse me. Is there a car park near here? ....

....

3. Excuse me. Is there a swimming pool in the town? ....

....

4. Excuse me. I'm looking for the post office. ....

....

5. Excuse me. Where's the police station, please? ....

....

2 Put in the correct preposition (*at, in, on, from, for, of*).

1. There are over 400 calories in 100g .... cheese.

2. 'Where are you ....?' 'San Francisco.'

3. She lives .... 37 Paradise Street.

4. Go straight on .... 600 yards.

5. I work .... the fifth floor.

6. This is a photo of my husband .... the beach.

7. Is there a fridge .... your kitchen?

8. This is a photo .... my family .... Canada.

9. 'Thank you very much.' 'Not .... all.'

10. 'Please sit down. Now, a few questions.'
    'Yes, ... course.'

3 Say these words with the correct stress.

police   office   station
supermarket   manager
downstairs   window
tomato   banana   car park
swimming pool   second
orange   potato

4 Read this with a dictionary.

Town's new swimming pool

They recently built a new swimming pool in the small town of Winter Park, Florida. It is one metre deep at one end and 55 metres deep at the other. That was not the original plan: half the pool has been eaten by an enormous hole.

The hole has also eaten two businesses, a house, five cars, several trees, and a large piece of road. It was still growing yesterday.

Mrs Mae Rose Owens was the first person to see it, last Friday. As she looked out of her window she saw a tree getting shorter and shorter. 'Suddenly the earth just opened up and down this tree went. I couldn't believe it.'

By 4 a.m. on Saturday, Mrs Owens had seen her home disappear, together with the buildings of a Porsche agent and a printing firm.

By Sunday, the hole had eaten one side of Denning Avenue, and was approaching three more houses. Yesterday it measured 400 metres across and 55 metres deep. According to Mr Jim Smoot, of the US Hydrological Survey, it will probably go on growing for several weeks. There is about 15 metres of water in the bottom.

The hole seems to be a result of the drought. Underground streams have dried out, making the subsoil contract.

(from *The Guardian*–adapted)

Unit 8C

C Where are they?

1 Complete the dialogue.

A: ....

B: Hello. Could I speak to Sally, please?

A: ....
   ....?

B: This is Jim. ....?

A: Fine, thanks. ....?

B: .... Would you like to have dinner with me at the Alhambra restaurant this evening?

A: That would be very nice. ....?

B: How about eight o'clock?

A: OK. Where's the Alhambra restaurant?

B: Near the station. When you come out of the
   station, ...
   ....
   ....
   ....

A: OK. See you this evening. Bye.

B: ....

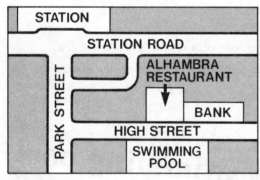

2 Vocabulary revision. Which word is different?

1. at   by   near   (go)   on
2. station   car park   orange   bank   police station
3. travel   bus   car   train   bicycle
4. what   this   who   where   how
5. cow   sheep   horse   dog   duck
6. live   home   stop   start   work
7. bedroom   toilet   kitchen   floor   living room
8. Thursday   think   three   thank you   bath
9. two   three   four   ten   twelve   twenty
   a thousand

3 Read the text, and then put the names of the rooms on the plan.

There are three rooms downstairs: a big *living room*, a fairly big *kitchen* opposite the living room, and a very small *dining room*. There's also a *toilet* opposite the stairs.

The bedrooms are upstairs. *John and Mary's bedroom* is at the top of the stairs on the right; the *bathroom* is opposite their room, and the *toilet* is next to the bathroom. Next to John and Mary's bedroom is *the children's bedroom*. The *spare bedroom* is at the end of the passage on the left.

UPSTAIRS

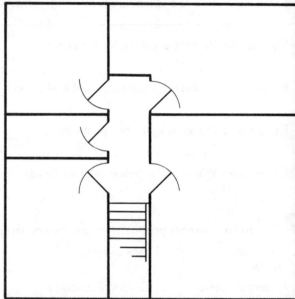

DOWNSTAIRS

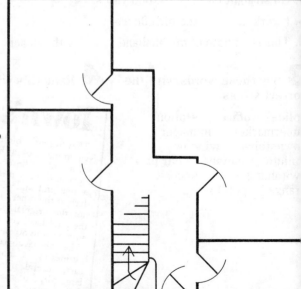

32

D I'm hungry

1 Say these sentences with the correct stress.

Excuse me. **Where's** the **near**est **post** office?
I'm **sorry**. I **don't know**.
Over **there** on the **right**.
John's at the cinema.
Mary's at **school**.

2 Make questions.

1. where | your wife | work?
Where does your wife work?

2. what | your | name?
....

3. you | like | beer?
....

4. you | got | any children?
....

5. Harry | like | school?
....

6. what newspaper | Helen | read?
....

7. what sort of books | the children | like?
....

8. you | hungry?
....

3 Vocabulary revision. What are these?

1. *Britain* ....   2. *an artist* ....   3. ....   4. ....   5. ....

6. ....   7. ....   8. ....   9. ....   10. ....

 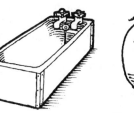 

11. ....   12. ....   13. ....   14. ....

33

4 Read this with a dictionary.

Dr Wagner and Judy are on their way to the airport in Dr Wagner's car. There is another car behind them, with a pretty blue lamp on top. Dr Wagner accelerates, and the police car disappears.

'But what's the problem, Judy?' asks Dr Wagner.

'I can't explain,' says Judy. 'It's too complicated.'

'I know what it is,' says Dr Wagner. 'It's that Sam. I don't like him at all. He's a very dishonest young man.'

'Sam is my boyfriend,' says Judy, 'and I love him. He has sensitive eyes and beautiful hands.'

Dr Wagner does not answer.

The World

 A How people live

1 Make at least six sentences.

In Italy
In Britain
In China
etc.

people often eat
people often drink

tea.
spaghetti.
rice.
etc.

....
....
....
....
....
....
....

2 Write a few sentences for an Amazon Indian, to tell him/her how you live.

....
....
....
....
....
....
....
....

3 Read this. Find the underlined words in a dictionary.

If you are invited to an English home, at five o'clock in the morning you get a cup of tea. You must not say 'Go away'. On the contrary, you have to say, with your best five o'clock smile: 'Thank you so much. I love a cup of early morning tea, especially early in the morning.'

Then you have tea for breakfast; then you have tea at eleven o'clock in the morning; then after lunch; then you have tea for tea; then after supper; and again at eleven o'clock at night.

You must not refuse tea under the following circumstances: if it is hot; if it is cold; if you are tired; if anybody thinks that you might be tired; if you are nervous; if you are happy; before you go out; if you are out; if you have just returned home; if you have had no tea for some time; if you have just had a cup.

You definitely must not follow my example. I sleep at five o'clock in the morning; I have coffee for breakfast; I drink innumerable cups of black coffee during the day.

The other day, for instance, I wanted a cup of coffee and a piece of cheese for tea. It was a very hot day, and my wife made some cold coffee and put it in the refrigerator, where it froze[1] solid. On the other hand, she left[2] the cheese on the kitchen table, where it melted. So I had a piece of coffee and a glass of cheese.

(from *How to be an Alien* by George Mikes – adapted)

[1]past of *freeze*
[2]past of *leave*

4 Try the crossword puzzle.

<ACROSS>

2. For people from the West, Chinese is .... to learn.
6. Jane doesn't eat meat, ... she eats a lot of fish.
8. Please .... down; Ms Brook will be here in a moment.
9. Turn .... and go straight on for 20 yards.
0. It's the third house on .... right.
2. .... you like bananas?
3. I like dogs, but my wife hates ....

14. 'Steve and Maria? Well, she's a very nice person, but I don't like .... much.'
17. Tom is not very tall, but the .... of my brothers are over six feet.
19. Tea .... coffee?
20. 'Hello, Jack.' '..........., Tony.'
21. The Amazon Basin is very ....
24. 'Where's Debbie?' 'Oh, she's at .... today – she's not well.'

D
O
W
N

1. Not clean.
2. You are on the third floor. The second floor is ....
3. Cats like this.
4. Opposite of *2 down*.
5. After all that work, I'm very ....
7. Opposite of *happy*.
11. 'Are you American?' 'Yes, I ....'
15. ...., you, him, her, it.
16. In a desert it's ....
18. Same as *13 across*.
19. She lives .... the sixth floor.
22. He lives .... Beaumont.
23. ....! Where's my car?

(Solution on page 127.)

B What do parrots eat?

1 How sure are you? Use *I know / I'm sure / definitely / certainly / perhaps / I think / I don't think / I don't know if.* Examples:

'I'm sure / I know / I think Sofia is in Bulgaria.'
'Perhaps Sofia is in Bulgaria.'
'Sofia is certainly/definitely in Bulgaria.'
'I don't think Sofia is in Bulgaria.'

'I'm sure / I know Sofia is not in Bulgaria.'
'Sofia is definitely/certainly not in Bulgaria.'
'I don't know if Sofia is in Bulgaria.'

1. Crocodiles live in rivers. ....
2. Snakes can dance. ....
3. There are no snakes in Ireland. ....
4. Australians speak English. ....
5. Austrians speak German. ....
6. A marathon is about 30 km long. ....
7. There are elephants in Brazil. ....
8. New York is the capital of the USA. ....
9. Rio de Janeiro is the capital of Argentina. ....
0. The Pope speaks English. ....
1. Shakespeare was Scottish. ....
2. The Kama Sutra is a well-known Indian restaurant in New York. ....
....
(Answers on page 127.)

35

2 Reading for information. Look at the three texts quickly and find the answers to these questions.

1. How many eggs does an emperor penguin lay? ....

2. How many kilograms does a big male gorilla weigh? ....

3. Where do gorillas sleep? ....

4. Do gorillas like snakes? ....

5. What do robins eat? ....

6. How many eggs do robins lay? ....

7. Do robins live in Scotland? ....

3 Reading for details. Read one of the texts with a dictionary.

A long wait

The female emperor penguin lays only one egg each year. She gives it to the male, who puts it on his feet and covers it with a special pouch. The female then goes to the sea, perhaps many kilometres from the male, and does not return for three months. The male stands in the cold, with no food. When the egg hatches, the female comes back and her thin, weak mate goes off to feed.

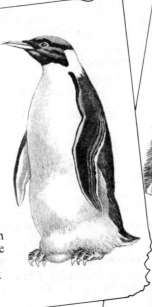

Facts about gorillas

1. A big male gorilla can weigh 200 kilograms.
2. Gorillas build a nest to sleep in each night.
3. A big gorilla's hands are 2.65 metres from its shoulders.
4. Gorillas live in groups and only move about one third of a mile a day.
5. Gorillas are afraid of snakes.
6. Gorillas never have fleas.

The robin

The robin is a plump brown bird 5½ inches (14cm) long. It has a red face and breast and a white belly. Males and females look alike, but the amount of red on the breast varies in individual birds.

Robins live all over Great Britain and Ireland, and are often found in gardens. Each male or pair has a territory which the male defends.

Robins eat fruit, worms and insects. The female lays four to six eggs in a nest made of moss and hair. The eggs are white with light red spots.

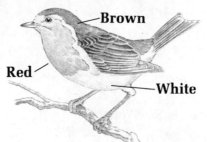

Brown

Red

White

4 Grammar revision. Put the words in the right order.

1. live   do   penguins   where   ?
2. don't   grass   snakes   eat   .
3. think   insects   don't   eat   cats
   I   that   .
4. India   live   tigers   in   do   ?
5. eat   cats   and   meat   fish
   certainly   .

CD The weather

1 Say these words.

fish   meat   this   in   wind   six   eat   it
It is in the kitchen.
America   Canada   China   Japan   Morocco   Brazil

2 Put in *often, quite often, sometimes, occasionally* or *never.*
(Tell the truth!)

1. I eat bananas. ....
2. I go to the cinema. ....
3. I drink whisky. ....
4. I speak French. ....
5. I work at home. ....
6. I get up before six o'clock. ....
....
7. I eat fish. ....
8. I go dancing. ....
9. I drink tea. ....
10. I read poetry. ....
11. I am bored. ....
12. I am unhappy. ....

3 Write a few sentences about the weather
in your country.

4 Read this with a dictionary. The first
time you read it, only look up the <u>underlined</u>
words in your dictionary.

Nearly three quarters of the <u>earth</u> is <u>covered</u>
with water. Water <u>heats up</u> more <u>slowly</u> than
land, but once it is warm it takes longer to cool
down. On the <u>moon</u>, where there is no water,
the temperature at night <u>falls</u> quite <u>quickly</u> and
night is much colder than day. This also happens
in inland deserts, hundreds of miles from any
sea. The climate of the <u>continents</u>, especially in
the temperate zones, is very much <u>affected</u> by
the <u>oceans</u> around them. The areas close to the
sea have a 'maritime climate', with rather cool
summers and warm winters. The interiors, far
from the sea, have a 'continental climate' with
extremely hot summers and cold winters.

(from *Penguin Book of the Physical World*)

It's a long story

PART 7

5 Read this with a dictionary.

'Single to Rio de Janeiro,
please,' says Judy.
    'First class or tourist?'
    'Oh, tourist, please.'
    Judy checks in and goes
through passport control to
the departure gate. On the
plane, she finds a seat by
the window. A young man
comes and sits down by
her. Judy looks at him. He
is tall and dark, about 25,
and very well dressed. Judy
is not interested in him.
    He has dark brown eyes,
a straight nose, a wide
humorous mouth, and
strong brown hands with
long sensitive fingers. He is
incredibly handsome. Judy
looks out of the window.

Appearances

A Sheila has got long dark hair

1 Put in *have got ('ve got)* or *has got ('s got)*.

1. Mrs Calloway .... short grey hair.

2. 'Where's the station?' 'I'm sorry. I .... no idea.

3. You .... beautiful eyes, Veronica.

4. We .... a nice house in a village near Coventry.

5. There is a man in Philadelphia who .... 26 names.

6. Some Eskimo languages .... hundreds of words for 'snow'.

7. Denmark .... no mountains.

8. My mother .... fair hair.

9. My brother and father .... dark hair.

2 Put in *and* if necessary.

1. Her hair is long *and* dark.

2. She has got long .... dark hair.

3. My boyfriend is tall .... intelligent.

4. Gillian has got a nice .... good-looking boyfriend.

5. I live in a large .... industrial town.

6. Peter's eyes are small .... green.

7. My flat is small .... dark.

8. Alex has got big .... brown eyes.

3 Put in *what, where, who, which* or *how*.

1. .... is your name?

2. .... is the station?

3. 'Hello. Could I speak to Alex?' 'Yes, ...'s that?' 'This is Lucy.'

4. .... time is it, please?

5. .... platform for Cardiff?

6. '............ do you do?' 'I'm an artist.'

7. '............ far is London from Liverpool?'

8. '............ are you?' 'Fine, thanks.'

9. '............ are you?' 'My name's Colin Watson.'

4 Read this with a dictionary. The first time you read, only look up the <u>underlined</u> words in your dictionary.

Thunder storms leave trail of chaos

By Aileen Ballantyne

SEVERE thunder storms caused <u>flooding</u>, lightning damage, impassable roads and a blocked <u>rail</u> line in the southern half of Britain yesterday.

The storms moved across England from the Bay of Biscay, heading north through the day.

In Devon and Dorset, <u>emergency</u> services received hundreds of calls from people whose homes had been flooded. At Charmouth, Dorset, 44 children and six adults had to be <u>evacuated</u> from a <u>camp</u> <u>site</u> when the <u>River</u> Axe burst its banks.

At Weymouth, the storms put a shopping centre under a foot of water last night and in north and west London <u>fire</u> <u>brigade</u> services had "hundreds of calls". Sewers

at Southall and Hanwell collapsed.

The West Sussex fire brigade said they received so many calls that firemen were dealing only with emergencies where <u>life</u> was at <u>risk</u>.

In the West Country, fallen trees as well as water made many roads impassable. In Sussex, Hampshire, and Kent, main roads were impassable, and <u>speed limits</u> had to be introduced on parts of the M4 and M1.

In Golders Green in London, three people were <u>slightly</u> <u>hurt</u> when their home was badly damaged by lightning and homes in Sway in Hampshire, Tunbridge Wells in Kent, and Denham in Buckinghamshire were hit.

(from The Guardian)

I JUST DISCOVERED WHY I'M SO CLUMSY. ...I'VE GOT 10 TOES.

©Field Enterprises, Inc., 1981

.. EVERYBODY HAS TEN TOES!

SEVEN ON ONE FOOT AND 3 ON THE OTHER?

B A red sweater and blue jeans

1 What colour are these?

   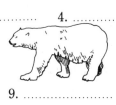

  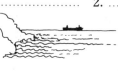

1. .... 2. .... 3. .... 4. ....

5. .... 6. .... 7. .... 8. .... 9. ....

2 Put in *am, are, is, have got* or *has got*.

1. I .... a small flat in London.

2. A Renault 4 .... a small car, but it .... four doors.

3. Where .... my trousers?

4. Her hair .... long and black and beautiful.

5. A spider .... eight legs.

6. Jane and Isaac .... four small children.

7. My father .... a big black dog.

8. There .... some beer in the fridge, I think.

9. Los Angeles .... on the west coast of the United States.

10. .... there any people from Germany in the class?

11. Lucy .... two boyfriends. They .... called Sam and Alec, and they .... both very nice.

12. An elephant .... big ears and a long nose (called a *trunk*).

3 Put the words in the correct order.

1. blue have small a car we got ....

2. green yellow and I a dress am wearing ....

3. dark has long Jane hair got ....

4. ears have grey big got elephants ....

5. TV colour a and chairs green dark two are there living room my in ....

6. green ears , Sally long eyes has small hair and got ....

4 Read two or more of these advertisements with a dictionary.

YOUNG MAN, lonely, wishes to meet warm, attractive woman, for friendship etc. Box G427.

EDINBURGH (m.) research worker, 25, not tall, shy, half Jew, half Arab, sincere, seeks interesting young lady. Box G382.

MAN, 23, Edinburgh, tall, intelligent, seeks female companion for genuine friendship. Enjoys theatre, music and travelling. Box G276.

MALE, 28, sks warm relationship slim, kind, gentle understanding woman, 30-50. Box G448.

DAD, 30, widower; and baby seek female friend, wkends & holidays. N. Yorkshire. Box G732.

WOMAN, mid-sixties, seeks male companion, similar age. East Devon area. Box G512.

ATTRACTIVE, intelligent lady, mid-forties, seeks single, compassionate man, similar age, to talk, laugh with. Box G735.

UNATTACHED LADY, 45, not particularly attractive seeks ordinary man, 53/58. Surrey/Sussex, for happy relationship. Box G795.

FAT, FEMALE LECTURER, dyed hair, young fifties, once married, seeks humorous, tolerant, sincere man, for living-it-up. Arts, gardening, home-life. Box G30.

AFRICAN JOURNALIST, 35, 5'5'', handsome and slim-built, seeks attractive London-based, warm, intellectual fun-loving prof female, 22-30, for lasting friendship. Will appreciate photos & phone number. Box G398.

TALL, GOOD-LOOKING DIVORCEE, forties, works in London, lives in country, interested in home life, walking, books and music, would like to meet unattached, caring, warm-natured man up to 60. Box G55.

SMALL, FRIENDLY, intelligent, red-headed designer, nearer 40 than 30, would like to meet man, over 28, black or white, warm-hearted, cheerful, hopefully non-smoking. Box G908.

ELEGANT, black divorcee, slim, 48, no children, wishes to meet tall, refined gentleman, 55-70, friendship/marriage. Midlands. Box G835.

TALL, SLIM, dark eyed Jewish widow, youthful, 49. Private Secretary. Sensitive, non-smoker, atheist, socialist, vegetarian, feminist, affectionate. Enjoys the arts, life, Woody Allen. Otherwise quite normal. Wish to meet male counterpart but who, unlike me, is solvent. Greater London. Box G31.

C I look like my father

1 Write the contractions.

she is ...*she's*........   he has got *he's got*....   I have not got *I haven't got*......

we are ....   John has got ....

you have got ....   John has not got ....

we have not got ....   they have ....

it is not ....   you are ....

John is ....   · it is ....

2 Make questions.

1. your mother | a car? *Has your mother got a car?*

2. she | a sister? ...*Has she got a sister?*

3. your parents | a nice house? ....

4. you | any cigarettes? ....

5. Mrs Hawkins | any children? ....

6. your house | a dining room? ....

7. you | a colour TV? ....

3 Make these sentences negative.

1. She's got blue eyes. *She hasn't got blue eyes.*

2. I've got some Italian friends. *I haven't got any Italian friends.*

3. We've got a garage. *We haven't got a garage.*

4. My parents have got a very nice house. ....

5. I've got some bread in my bag. ....

6. Peter and Ellen have got a Rolls-Royce. ....

7. Sally has got long hair. ....

8. Robert has got his father's nose. ....

9. I've got my mother's personality. ....

4 Write a description of yourself or a friend.

....

....

....

....

....

....

....

....

D | What a nice shirt!

1 Complete the dialogue.

A: What's your new girlfriend like, John?

B: Oh, she's very ....

She's got .... and

....

A: Oh yes? Has she got a sister?

B: Yes, but her sister doesn't look like her at all.

She's ...., and she's got

....

A: Really? What's her .... number?

2 Complete these sentences.

1. What .... shirt!

2. What .... shoes!

3. I .... ear-rings.

4. .... are nice trousers.

5. .... 's a very pretty ring.

6. What .... blouse!

3 Make compliments about these articles of clothing.

What nice jeans!

....

....

4 Read this with a dictionary.

It's a long story PART 8

'Excuse me. Would you like a drink?'

'Oh, er, yes. Thank you very much. A whisky, please.'

The young man gave[1] Judy her drink and smiled at her. He had[2] an incredibly attractive smile. He really looked very nice: calm, friendly and kind. 'Perhaps he's a doctor,' she thought[3] – 'a surgeon, with those strong sensitive hands. Or perhaps an artist, or a musician.' Yes, he looked like an artist. She looked at him again and smiled.

'What time is it, please?' he asked.

Judy looked at her watch. 'Two thirty-five.'

'Thank you,' he said, and smiled at her. She smiled back at him. He smiled again. He took[4] a gun out of his pocket, stood[5] up, and walked to the front of the plane.

[1]*gave*: past of *give*   [4]*took*: past of *take*
[2]*had*: past of *have*   [5]*stood*: past of *stand*
[3]*thought*: past of *think*

Personal history

A He was born in London

1 Who did what? Write sentences.

Indira Gandhi	made several famous films, including *The Birds* and *Psycho*.
Gauguin	received the Nobel Prize for literature in 1925.
Agatha Christie	
George Bernard Shaw	worked as an engineer in Berne.
Karl Marx	was born in Allahabad in 1917.
Hitchcock	died in London in 1883.
Einstein	lived in Tahiti for several years.
	wrote several detective stories.

2 Read these notes and then write a few sentences about Hemingway's life.

Ernest Hemingway b. Illinois 1899, d. Idaho 1961. Father doctor, mother musician and painter. Ambulance driver in Italy during First World War. Journalist in Paris after war for several years. Many well-known novels, including *The Sun Also Rises, Farewell to Arms, For Whom the Bell Tolls, The Old Man and the Sea*. Nobel Prize for literature 1954.

3 Write a few sentences about your life, or the life of a famous man or woman.

B They didn't drink tea

1 When Jake was 20 he was very poor, and life was difficult. He had to work very hard. But he had a good time. Now he's 40. He has plenty of money and a very good job. Life is easy. And he still has a good time!

THEN

Jake worked very hard.
He lived in one small room.
He started work at 7.30.
....
He ate cheap food.
....
He did not travel much.
He played football on Saturday afternoons.
....
....
His mother worked in a shop.
....

NOW

He doesn't work very hard.
He lives in a very big house.
....
He works five hours a day.
....
He often goes to restaurants.
....
He still has a lot of girlfriends.
He doesn't want to be an artist.
....
He's got three cars.

2 Imagine you are old and rich. Write about your life now, and your life when you were young.

3 Use your dictionary to read this; but ONLY look up the <u>underlined</u> words.

Childhood in an Indian Village

Going back as far as I can remember as a child in an Indian community, I had no sense of knowing about the other people around me except that we were all somehow <u>equal</u>.... There was only one class. Nobody was interested in getting on <u>top</u> of anybody else.

You could see it in our <u>games.</u> Nobody organized them. There weren't any <u>competitive</u> sports. But we were involved in lots of activity (I was not like I am now; I was in pretty good shape at that time) and we were organized, but not in the sense that there were ways of finding out who had won and who had lost. We played <u>ball</u> like everyone else, but no one kept <u>score.</u> Even if we did formally compete in the games we played, no one was a winner though someone may have won. It was only the moment. If you beat someone by pulling a <u>bow</u> and <u>arrow</u> and shooting the arrow <u>further</u>, it only meant that you shot the arrow further at that moment. That's all it lasted. It didn't mean you were better in any way whatsoever. It just meant that at that particular time the arrow went further; maybe it was just the way you let the bow go. These kinds of things are very important to me and that is why I am talking about them.

One of the very important things was the relationship we had with our families. We didn't always live at home. We lived wherever we happened to be at that particular time when it got dark. If you were two or three miles away from home, then that is where you slept.

People would feed you even if they didn't know who you were. We'd spend an evening, perhaps, with an old <u>couple</u>, and they would tell us stories. Most of these stories were <u>legends</u>, and they were told to us mostly in the <u>winter</u> time. In the <u>summer</u> people would generally take us out and we would do a number of things which in some way would allow us to learn about life and what it was all about: that is, by talking about some particular person and demonstrating what that person did. In all the years I spent there, I don't remember anyone teaching us anything.

Wilfred Pelletier
(from *This Book is about Schools*)

C Danced till half past one

1 Express these times in another way.

3.15 *a quarter past three* 9.20 .... 5.15 ....
7.40 .... 11.55 .... 9.25 ....
3.35 .... 5.30 .... 7.05 ....
10.45 .... 6.10 .... 1.50 ....

2 Make questions.

1. He was born in 1919. *When was he born?* ....

2. He lived in Vienna. ....

3. He worked in a bank. ....

4. He wrote seven novels. ....

5. He had three children. ....

6. His father died in 1932. ....

7. He went to America in 1936. ....

3 Write a few sentences about what you did yesterday or last weekend.

4 Decide which sentences belong to the story about Queen Elizabeth I, and which sentences belong to the story about Princess Grace. Use a dictionary if you want. Write out the two stories.

a. Grace Kelly was born on the east coast of the United States in 1929.
b. Queen Elizabeth I was the daughter of Henry VIII and his second wife, Anne Boleyn.
c. When she was three months old she went to live at Hatfield, far from the King and Queen.
d. Her mother was executed by her father when the little girl was two and a half years old.
e. When she was 21, she went to Hollywood and began acting in films.
f. The young princess learnt Italian, French, Latin and Greek from royal tutors.
g. She appeared in the film *High Noon*, and won an Academy Award ('Oscar') for her acting in *A Country Girl*
h. In 1956 she married Prince Rainier of Monaco.
i. She followed her half-brother Edward and her half-sister Mary to the throne.
j. She then retired from her career in America and devoted herself to her royal duties.
k. She never married, and ruled for 45 years as a strong and independent queen.
l. She breastfed her own babies, and publicly encouraged other mothers to do the same.
m. She was much loved by the people of England, and her reign was one of power and glory for her country.
n. She died in 1982 after a car accident.

D Who wrote to Alice?

1 What is the past of each verb?

marry *married*	know	help
want	come	get
study	stop	tell
have	hate	shop

2 What is the infinitive of each verb?

heard *hear*	died	did
woke	said	liked
worked	could	went
called	finished	

3 Write questions for these answers.

1. In Vienna. *Where were you born?*
2. Yesterday morning.
3. My sister.
4. John did.
5. She loved Barry.
6. By car.
7. The blue one.
8. Bacon and eggs.
9. On the beach.
10. Seven.

4 Read this with a dictionary.

'Good afternoon. This is your hijacker speaking. We are now flying at 550 miles per hour at a height of 29,000 feet. In approximately one and a half hours we will be over the north of Scotland. I wish you a pleasant flight.'

Judy's head was going round and round. First Sam, then the police, and now the hijacker. Where would it all end? Life was really much too complicated. She drank her whisky. It didn't make any difference. She looked out of the window. The sky was full of big dark clouds. So was her head.

Some time later the plane started going down. The pilot's door opened, and the hijacker came out, still holding his gun. He walked up to her and smiled. 'You know,' he said, 'you really are extremely beautiful. Come and put on your parachute.' Judy fainted.

It's a long story PART 9

Buying things

A This one?

1 Complete the sentences.

CUSTOMER: *Could* you *show* me those ear-rings, please?

SHOP ASSISTANT: .... ?

CUSTOMER: No, the .... in front of those.

SHOP ASSISTANT: .... ?

CUSTOMER: Yes.

SHOP ASSISTANT: .... are.

——◇——

CUSTOMER: .... I see .... watch, please?

SHOP ASSISTANT: The .... behind the spoons?

CUSTOMER: Yes, please.

SHOP ASSISTANT: Of ....

2 Complete the sentences.

1. Could | show | book | please? *Could you show me that book, please?*

2. Could | see | watch | right | please? ....

3. Are | any ear-rings | box? ....

4. Could | read me | word? ....

5. Is | your car | front | house? ....

6. Were | any children | front | shop? ....

45

3 Write some sentences about this picture.

There's a shirt in front of the bicycle.

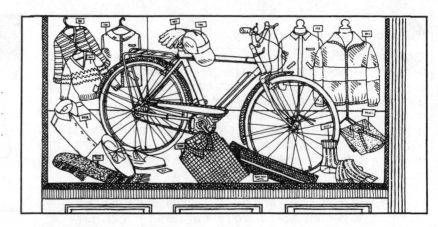

4 Try the crossword puzzle.

ACROSS

1. 'Where's Bob?' 'Jane took .... to the station at three o'clock.'
3. I .... to work by bus.
4. Dumfries is in the .... of Scotland.
7. 'What does Judy do?' '............ is a medical student.'
8.
9. It's over there .... the reception desk.
10. Where .... I find a newspaper?
13. 'Could I see that, please?' 'Of course. .... you are.'

DOWN

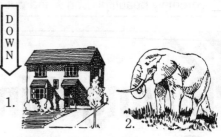

1.

2.

3. The same as *3 across*.
5. Susan and Colin are doctors. .... live in Dundee.
6. Judy is in London, but .... boyfriend is in Brazil.
8. Where can I .... cigarettes?
9. The opposite of *girl*.
10. Excuse me. Where's the nearest .... park?
11. Where .... your shoes?
12. ....! I can't find my keys!

(Solution on page 127.)

B Yellow doesn't suit me

1 Answer the questions.

Use some of these words.

| large | small | modern | old | comfortable | cheap | expensive | good-looking |
| kind | nice | long | round | oval | red | black | brown | green | etc. |

1. What colour car would you like? (**Answer:** A .... one.)

2. What sort of house would you like? ....

3. What colour shirt/blouse/tee-shirt/etc. are you wearing now? ....

4. What sort of watch have you got? ....

5. What sort of dinner do you usually have? ....

6. What sort of face have you got? ....

46

2 Put in *I, me, it, you, they, them.*

1. Excuse .... Where can .... buy stamps?

2. .... look like my father, and my children look like ....

3. Can you meet .... at the station at eight o'clock?

4. Your trousers fit .... very well, but .... don't suit ....

5. 'What did you think of the film last night?' 'I liked ....'

6. I love .... Do .... love ....?

7. 'We've got some very nice rings.' 'Oh, yes? Could I see ....?'

8. ....'s eight o'clock.

9. 'How are your parents?' '........... 're very well, thanks.' 'Say hello to .... from ....'

10. Would you like to have dinner with .... tonight?

11. These shoes look nice. Can I try .... on?

12. Look at my new ear-rings. Do you like ....?

3 What clothes are you wearing today? How well do they fit/suit you? Example:

My trousers fit me very well/fairly well; my shirt doesn't fit me very well.

C The next train to Oxford

1 Complete the dialogues.

A: I'd .... two returns to Rugby, ...

B: That's £17.40.

A: Thank you. .... is the next train, please?

B: To Rugby? There's one .... 10.15, ... at Crewe; or there's a .... one at 10.30, arriving .... 12.15.

A: .... platform for the 10.30?

B: .... 4.

A: Thank you very much.

———◇———

A: Where are you from?

B: ....?

A: Where are you from?

B: I'm sorry. I don't .... you .... more slowly, please?

A: What country are you ....? .... from Germany? .... France?

B: Oh, er – I'm Greek.

2 Say these sentences with the correct stress.

1. **Two sin**gles to **Rug**by, **please**.
2. **What time** is the **next train** to **Cam**bridge, **please**?
3. There's a di**rect train** at **six for**ty.
4. **Which plat**form?
5. **How** would you **like** it?
6. I'm **sorry**, I **don't** under**stand**. Could you **speak** more **slow**ly?

47

3 Find the answers to these questions in the text below. Don't read the complete text.

1. I missed the 12.10 to Cardiff from London. When is the next train to Cardiff?
   ....

2. If a second-class ticket to Birmingham costs £5, how much does a first-class ticket cost?
   ....

3. Is it possible to buy a Britrail Pass in Bristol?
   ....

4. Is is possible to buy a Britrail Seapass in the USA?
   ....

(from Hello Britain)

TRAVELLING BY TRAIN

British Rail operates a service of 16,000 trains a day serving over 2,000 stations; there's hardly a part of Britain that can't be reached by train. A fast Inter-City network links London with all major cities, such as Bristol, Cardiff, York and Edinburgh, with trains leaving the capital every hour during the main part of the day. Also, at no extra cost, you can travel up to 125 mph (200 kph) on the High Speed Inter-City Trains to many major destinations.

On most trains you have the choice between First or Second (Economy) Class. First Class seats are more spacious and cost 50% more than the Second Class fare. Many Inter-City trains have a full meals service, and grills, snacks and drinks are also available on other trains.

Buying your rail ticket

Overseas visitors are entitled to one of the best rail travel bargains anywhere – the Britrail Pass. It gives unlimited travel throughout Britain for 8, 15, 22 days or 1 month (7, 14, 21 days or 1 month in North America). Get one from Britrail Travel International Offices in North America or from local travel agents or major railway stations in Europe. Visitors from the Continent can also buy a Britrail Seapass. This covers all the facilities offered above, plus the return sea journey across the Channel. **Remember, these passes are not sold in Britain and must be bought before you leave your own country.**

Otherwise, in addition to the normal single return fares, certain tickets can be bought at reduced rates – see this page under heading "Lots of Travel Bargains". For general rail enquiries, go to your nearest British Rail Travel Centre or any railway station.

LOTS OF TRAVEL BARGAINS

How much you pay depends on where and when you want to

D Five hundred pounds for a month

1 Put one of these words in each blank.

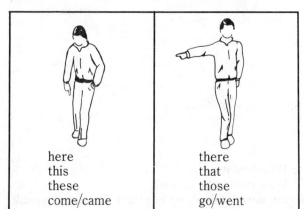

here	there
this	that
these	those
come/came	go/went

1. I .... here in 1975.

2. I go to .... hotel whenever I'm in Eastbourne.

3. I think .... people over there are Greek.

4. I don't understand .... sentence. Could you come .... and help me with it?

5. .... grapes are delicious. Would you like some?

6. 'Could I see .... newspaper for a minute?' 'Of course – .... you are.'

7. 'I love walking in the Himalayas.' 'Do you .... there often?'

2 Use five or more of these words to write some true sentences about yourself.

didn't	last night	woke	knew	came	went	lived	became

3 Answer these questions.

1. How are you? ....

2. What do you do? ....

3. Where's the nearest bus stop? ....

4. How many aunts have you got? ....

5. Where were you born? ....

6. Where is the capital of your country? ....

7. Are you hungry or thirsty or tired? ....

8. What floor is your bedroom on? ....

9. Is there a television in your room? ....

10. What do you usually have for lunch? ....

4 Read this with a dictionary.

Judy opened her eyes. The sun was shining, and a cool wind was blowing on her face. She felt very light and happy. 'Where am I?' she said. Behind her, a man's voice said '100 feet above Loch Ness. Can you swim?' Judy fainted again.

    When she opened her eyes, she was lying on the bank of the loch, with her head on her parachute. 'Allow me to introduce myself,' said the handsome young man. 'My name is Jasper MacDonald.' 'Why did you hijack the plane?' asked Judy. 'It's my birthday,' said Jasper. 'Now let's go to my castle and find some dry clothes.'

Differences

A   I can sing, but I can't draw

1 Say these sentences with the correct stress.

1. **Ba**bies **can't smile** when they're **born**.
2. **Most ba**bies can **smile** when they're **six weeks old**.
3. **How ma**ny languages can you **speak**?
4. Can **any** of you under**stand** Portu**guese**?
5. We can **drive** you **home** if you'd **like**.
6. '**Please show** me your **driving** licence.' 'I **can't**, it's at **home**.'
7. I **can't** under**stand** where **Jane** is.
8. 'Can you **hear** me?' 'Of **course** I **can!**'

2 Write five sentences about things you can do (say how well),
and five sentences about things you can't do. Examples:

I can swim very well.
I can sing a little.
I can't cook.

3 Past tense verbs: put an affirmative verb or *did not* in each blank.

Yesterday everything went wrong. My alarm clock *did not* ring, so I *was* late. I .... eat breakfast. I ran for the bus, but it .... early, so I missed it. When I got to the office, there .... a note from my supervisor on my desk. She wanted to see me. I .... to her office, but I .... want to go in, because there .... three important-looking people there. I left a note on her secretary's desk. But her secretary .... not at work, so the supervisor .... see the note. When she finally .... back to my desk in the afternoon, she .... not happy.

4 Strange but true. Use a dictionary if you need it.

Gorillas can't swim.
Mice can sing.
Horses can sleep standing up.
Elephants can't jump, and they can't remember things very well, but they can stand on their heads.
A male emperor moth can smell a female eleven kilometres away.
Leopold Stokowski could play the violin and the piano when he was five.
Thomas Young (an 18th-century scientist) could speak twelve languages when he was eight.
The Danish linguist Rasmus Rask could speak 235 languages.
The American tennis player Roscoe Tanner can serve a ball at 225 kilometres an hour.

B I can do anything better than you

1 In the following sentences, mark the stressed syllables like this: ⌢⌢

I can <u>drive</u> <u>bet</u>ter than my <u>bro</u>ther.

Then mark the vowels pronounced /ə/: *O*

I c(a)n <u>drive</u> <u>bet</u>t(e)r th(a)n my <u>bro</u>th(e)r.

1. My aunt can play tennis better than Billie Jean King.

2. I can sing any note higher than you.

3. I was good at football when I was younger.

4. When I was younger I couldn't swim at all.

2 Pronounce these words. If you have problems, look at page 59 in your Student's Book.

wake   cat   tall   map   past   saw   came

3 Fish can swim better than pigeons can fly better than squirrels can climb trees better than kangaroos can jump higher than horses can run faster than canaries can sing better than fish can swim...

Write a 'circle' like this about your family. Example:

I can run faster than my mother can cook better than my father can...

4 Read this, and try to answer the last question. You can use the table to help you.

'My four granddaughters are all very clever girls,' the bishop said. 'Each of them plays a different musical instrument and each can speak one European language as well as – if not better than – a native of the country.'

'What does Mary play?' asked someone.

'The cello.'

'Who plays the violin?'

'D'you know,' said the bishop, 'I've temporarily forgotten. But I know it's the girl who speaks French.'

The rest of the facts which I found out were of a rather negative kind. I learned that the organist is not Valerie; that the girl who can speak German is not Lorna; and that Mary knows no Italian. Anthea doesn't play the violin; nor is she the girl who speaks Spanish. Valerie knows no French; Lorna doesn't play the harp; and the organist can't speak Italian.

What can Valerie do?

(from *My Best Puzzles in Logic and Reasoning* by Hubert Phillips – adapted)

	cello	violin	organ	harp		French	German	Italian	Spanish
Mary	yes	no	no	no	Mary				
Valerie					Valerie				
Lorna					Lorna				
Anthea					Anthea				

(Solution on page 127.)

C I'm much taller than my mother

1 Write the comparative and superlative of:

pretty .... long ....
cold .... thirsty ....
young .... large ....
rude .... humid ....
hot .... tall ....
red .... warm ....
talkative ....
cheerful ....
sensitive ....

2 Write the simple forms of these comparative and superlative adjectives.

funnier .... oldest .... cheaper ....
nicest .... noisiest .... bigger ....
worse .... later ....
thinner .... smaller ....

3 Change the sentences as in the example.

1. I'm older than him. *He's younger than me.*

2. I'm taller than her. *She's shorter*

3. He's bigger than me. *I'm*

4. He's heavier than her. *lighter*

5. We're younger than you. ....

6. She's darker than me. ....

7. They're shorter than us. ....

4 Strange but true. Read this with a dictionary.

Blond beards grow faster than dark beards.
The most common family name in the world is Chang: there are about 75,000,000 people called Chang in China. The most common first name in the world is Mohammed.
The oldest map was made 5,000 years ago: it shows the River Euphrates.
Rats can live longer without water than camels.
Nearly three times as many people live in Mexico City as in Norway.
One of the narrowest streets in the world is St John's Lane, in Rome: it is 49cm wide. But there is a street in Cornwall, England, that is even narrower: it is 48cm wide at its narrowest point.
Loud – louder – loudest: you can hear alligators calling a mile away. You can hear the clock bell 'Big Ben' (on the Houses of Parliament, London) ten miles away. When the volcano Krakatoa erupted in 1883, it was heard 3,000 miles away.
Cold – colder – coldest: There was ice on the river Nile in 829 AD and 1010 AD. On average, New York is colder than Reykjavik (Iceland). The coldest place in the world, in Antarctica, has an average temperature of −57.8°C.

D The same or different?

1 In English, most three-syllable words have got this stress pattern: ▢□□ possible

In this list, there are three words with different stress patterns. Find the words and write them beside their stress patterns.

WORDS

comfortable   good-looking
anything   difficult
expensive   understand
interesting   happier
beautiful   easiest

Write the three different words here.

▢□▫ ....

□▢▫ ....

□□▢ ....

2 Write six sentences about yourself, using (not) as…as…. Examples:

I'm not as strong as a horse.
I can't run as fast as a rabbit.
I can play tennis as well as my brother.

52

3 Compare two people that you know very well. Write at least 100 words.

It's a long story
PART II

4 Read this with a dictionary.

It didn't take long to get to Jasper's castle. It was an enormous building, about half a mile from Loch Ness, with tall towers, battlements and a moat, and at least 200 rooms. 'What a place!' said Judy. 'Well, it's not much, but it's home,' said Jasper. 'Let me show you to your room. And I'll see if I can find you some of my sister's clothes.'

Judy's room was about ten minutes' walk from the main entrance, up a lot of stairs and along a lot of corridors. It was beautiful, decorated in light blue and lilac, with some wonderful pieces of antique furniture. There was a splendid view of the loch and the mountains. 'This is lovely!' said Judy. 'How many of you live here?' 'Just my sister and I,' said Jasper. 'And the ghost, of course. See you later.'

15

Some history

A 91 million years ago

1 Write down five things you like. Then write down beside each thing how long ago you did/had/enjoyed it. Examples:

running — three days ago
coffee — two hours ago

2 Write the infinitives of ten verbs you know. Do you know the past tense forms? Write them down if you do; if you don't, look them up in the dictionary, and write down what you learn.

INFINITIVE	PAST
1.	
2.	
3.	
4.	
5.	
6.	
7.	
8.	
9.	
10.	

3 Pronounce these sentences with the correct stress.

1. A **long time** ago, Africa was **not far** from **South** America.
2. **How long** ago was your **first English lesson?**
3. **How long** ago did Co**lum**bus dis**cov**er A**me**rica?
4. I **came** to this **coun**try **two years** ago.

4 Compare yourself and your life now and ten years ago. Write at least ten sentences.
Examples:

Ten years ago I lived in a flat; now I live in a house.
Ten years ago I weighed 55 kilos, and I still do.
I can run better than I could ten years ago.

B Where was Galileo born?

1 Stressed or not? Look at these sentences, and decide if *was* or *were* is stressed in each one. Underline *was* and *were* when they are stressed. Then read the sentences aloud.

1. **Who** was the **first man** on the **moon?**
2. Was **Gol**da **Meir born** in **Ru**ssia? **Yes**, she was.
3. **Hen**ry **Kiss**inger wasn't **born** in A**me**rica.
4. **Who** were the **Wright bro**thers? They were the **first men** to **fly** an **ae**roplane.
5. E**li**zabeth the **First** and **Ma**ry **Stu**art weren't **sis**ters; they were **cou**sins.
6. Were Pi**erre** and **Ma**rie **Cu**rie **phy**sicists? Of **course** they were.
7. Gali**le**o was the **son** of a musician.

2 Make questions.

1. Amelia Earhart took flying lessons when she was 22. Where *did she take flying lessons?*

2. Galileo lost the use of his eyes. When ....

....

3. Marie Curie was born in Warsaw. When ....

4. Ho Chi Minh once went to New York. How ....

5. Amelia Earhart once worked for the Red Cross. Where ....

....

6. Galileo's lectures were very famous. Why ....

....

7. Marie and Pierre Curie had a famous daughter. Who ....

....

54

3 Read the first text and its notes. Then read the second text and write notes for it.

Margareta Gertruida Zelle was born in Leeuwarden, in the Netherlands, in 1876. She married an army officer and went with him to Indonesia, where she learnt Javanese and Hindu dances. She went back to Europe, where she became a famous dancer, calling herself 'Mata Hari'. She was accused of being a spy for the Germans and was executed in Vincennes, in France, in 1917.

Margareta Gertruida Zelle (called 'Mata Hari')
– Dutch dancer
– Leeuwarden, 1876 – Vincennes, 1917
– husband: army officer
– learnt Javanese & Hindu dances in Indonesia
– back to Europe: famous
– executed as a German spy

Marco Polo was born in Venice in 1254. With his father and his uncle, who were businessmen, he travelled to China in 1275. They were the first Europeans to do this. Marco Polo stayed at the court of the Chinese emperor for many years, and went as an ambassador for the emperor to Tonkin, Annam, India and Persia. He went back to Venice in 1295, made rich by his travels. Polo wrote a book about his experiences, but not many people believed him at first. He died in 1324.

4 Write about someone from your country's history. OR: Write a short paragraph about your mother/grandfather/etc. as a child.

 America invades Britain!

1 Put one of these words in each blank.

had	broke	lost	came	began	went
made	took	put	knew	brought	

1. He .... to school in a very small village.

2. I .... home very late last night.

3. Charlie Chaplin .... seven children.

4. Sharon .... some photos to show us yesterday.

5. He said he was sorry, but I .... he wasn't.

6. I .... an aspirin half an hour ago, and my head's much better now.

7. She .... her glasses by sitting on them.

8. Yehudi Menuhin .... playing the violin when he was very young.

9. He .... a lot of noise when he was a child.

10. Joan .... six pounds last month.

11. I .... your magazine in the living room.

2 Put one of these in each blank.

then	as soon as	finally	so	still

1. I had a cup of tea and .... went straight to bed.

2. It was .... very dark when I left for work this morning.

3. The last people .... left the party at 1.30.

4. .... she comes home, could you ask her to phone me?

5. She told her mother first; .... she told her brothers and sisters.

6. She telephoned him .... she knew he was back from holiday.

7. She doesn't have a phone, ... I couldn't ring her.

3 Write sentences with *then, as soon as, finally, so* and *still* (one sentence with each).

4 Read these sentences; you can use a dictionary. Then put the sentences in order, to make two paragraphs of a story.

But Florence found parties boring; she wanted to be a nurse.

Then she was in charge of a nursing-home for women in London.

Florence Nightingale came from a rich family and was very pretty.

Finally, in 1850, when she was 30, her parents accepted her decision.

In her family, young girls usually spent their time going to parties until they married rich young men.

Soon she was asked to go to the Crimea to take charge of the wounded soldiers.

So she went to study in a hospital in Germany.

Forty per cent of the patients died.

By 1900 unsafe hospitals and ignorant nurses were things of the past.

The death rate dropped to two per cent.

The conditions in the Crimean hospital were terrible.

Workmen put in a proper drainage system and supplied pure drinking water.

Certain beds seemed fatal: soldiers died in them after two days.

She was an important force in the movement to reform hospitals and nursing in England.

On her return to England people greeted Florence Nightingale as a heroine.

Nightingale decided that this was because of bad drains, and insisted that the government do something about it.

——◇——

D Who? How? What? Where? Which?

1 Try the crossword puzzle.

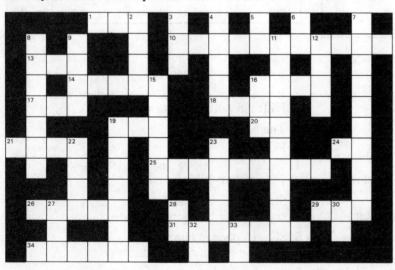

ACROSS

1. Where did you .... the bread, dear?
10. 'Was that television programme ....?' 'No, I fell asleep after ten minutes.'
13. How long .... did he leave?
14. I loved playing the guitar when I was younger, and I .... play occasionally.
16. He ran, and got on the train just as it began to ....
17. Past tense of *get*.
18. The new telephones are smaller .... the old ones.
19. I .... cook quite well, but I don't enjoy it.
20. Present tense of *did*.

56

21. Past tense of *go*.
24. I'm not quite .... tall .... my boyfriend.
25. The cooker was ...., but it cooks much better than the cheaper ones.
26. I always .... with a window open.
29. Present tense of *said*.
31. My cousins .... got here at ten o'clock in the evening – their plane was four hours late.
34. Some of us came by car, but the .... walked.

D O W N

2. Some people left early, but John and Carole stayed .... midnight.
3. 'When .... you leave school?' 'In 1975.'
4. When did you .... learning English?
5. Is your brother dark .... fair?
6. The same as *24 across*.
7. She's a student at Yale ....
8. In 1778, the British .... at the American navy.
9. I .... my keys yesterday, and I still can't find them.
11. My car is beautiful and fast, but it's not very ....; it uses a lot of petrol.

12. First she phoned her boyfriend, and .... she made a cup of tea.
15. Judy's hair is much .... than it was the last time I saw her.
16. Crazy.
19. 'Oh, look, this one is much ....! It's only £1.50.'
22. 'Can any of your sisters ....?' 'Yes, Joan's a secretary.'
23. Past tense of *begin*.
27. We've got a .... of beer, but we haven't got much wine.
28. On the night .... December 28, everyone in the village was home in bed.
30. Where were you .... midnight last Thursday?
32. Nairobi is the largest city .... Kenya.
33. 'Who's the oldest person here?' 'I ....'

(Solution on page 128.)

2 Read this with a dictionary.

It's a long story

PART 12

Judy had a bath, and then put on some of Jasper's sister's clothes. They fitted her perfectly. She looked at herself in the mirror, smiled, frowned, and went downstairs.

'Hello,' said Jasper. 'Did I tell you how beautiful you are?'

'Yes, you did,' said Judy.

'Fine,' said Jasper. 'Let me show you round the castle before tea.'

'But I don't want to stay for tea,' said Judy.

'This part of the castle was built in 1480,' said Jasper.

'I want to go to Rio,' said Judy.

'This is a portrait of my ancestor Donald MacDonald,' said Jasper.

'I want to see my boyfriend Sam,' said Judy.

'He was a friend of King James VI,' said Jasper.

'I love him,' said Judy.

'James VI?' said Jasper, interested.

'No, you fool,' said Judy. 'My boyfriend Sam.'

'Oh, Sam Watson,' said Jasper. 'You don't want to see him.'

'Yes, I do,' said Judy.

'No, you don't,' said Jasper. 'This is a portrait of my ancestor MacDonald MacDonald.'

'How do you know Sam?' said Judy.

'He was a friend of King Robert the Bruce,' said Jasper.

'Sam?' said Judy.

'No, you fool,' said Jasper. 'MacDonald. You don't want to see Sam. You want to stay here with me. I love you.'

Out of a door came an old man with white hair and very strange clothes. He was carrying his head under his arm. He looked very like the portrait.

'Who's that?' asked Judy.

'The ghost,' said Jasper.

'You don't want to go and see Sam,' said the ghost. 'You want to stay here with Jasper.'

57

Personal information

A Ages, heights and weights

1 Complete the dialogue.

DOCTOR: ...., Mr Rannoch?

PATIENT: Five feet ten, Doctor.

DOCTOR: Yes, I see. And ....?

PATIENT: About a hundred and eighty pounds.

DOCTOR: Yes, right. ....?

PATIENT: Thirty-two.

2 Write sentences.

Example:

Beryl Jones is nineteen. She is five feet five inches tall, and weighs a hundred and forty-two pounds.

NAME	AGE	HEIGHT	WEIGHT
Beryl Jones	19	5'5"	142lbs
Oscar Duke	37	6'1"	190lbs
Tony Lands	14	5'2"	103lbs
Amelia Berry	68	5'4"	98lbs
Oliver Ashe	33	5'10"	230lbs

3 Strange but true. Read this with a dictionary.

Human fossils found in Tanzania are about 3,500,000 years old.

There is a tree in California that is 4,600 years old.

A sequoia tree in California is 272ft (83m) tall, and 79ft (24m) round. It contains enough wood to make 500,000,000 matches.

A cat in Devon lived to the age of 36.

On June 19, 1944, a dog in Pennsylvania had 23 puppies.

A blue whale can measure 110ft 2½in (33.58m) long, and weigh 187 tons.

Living bacteria dating from 1,500 years ago have been found in a Cumbrian lake.

The eye of a giant squid is 15 inches (38cm) across.

Cheetahs can run at up to 63 miles an hour (101 km an hour).

The three-toed sloth (found in tropical America) travels at 8ft (2.44m) a minute when it is in a hurry.

(from the *Guinness Book of Records*)

B You look shy

1 Put in *some* or *any*.

1. I'd like .... tomatoes, please.

2. Are there .... French people in your class?

3. Is there .... cheese in the fridge?

4. There were .... nice people at the party last night.

5. I'm sorry. We haven't got .... steak.

2 Put in *a/an* or *the* where necessary.

1. What's ...*the*... time?

2. My brother's ...*an*... architect.

3. I like ...—... steak, but I don't like .... eggs.

4. She lives in .... nice flat on .... fifth floor of .... old house.

5. Today's .... thirteenth of December.

6. Mary is .... John's sister.

7. What is .... your address?

8. It's terrible – .... eggs are £1.80 .... dozen.

9. What time is .... next train for Glasgow, please?

10. I'd like half .... litre of .... red wine.

3 Write a few sentences about your appearance and personality. Example:

I am quite shy. I look calm, but actually I am rather nervy. I think I am kind, but sometimes I am bad-tempered. I think I look like a businessman.

4 Read this with a dictionary. Which is the picture of Leamas?

Leamas was a short man with close, iron-grey hair, and the physique of a swimmer. He was very strong. This strength was discernible in his back and shoulders, in his neck, and in the stubby formation of his hands and fingers.

He had a utilitarian approach to clothes, as he did to most other things, and even the spectacles he occasionally wore had steel rims. Most of his suits were of artificial fibre, none of them had waistcoats. He favoured shirts of the American kind with buttons on the points of the collars, and suede shoes with rubber soles.

He had an attractive face, muscular, and a stubborn line to his thin mouth. His eyes were brown and small; Irish, some said. He looked like a man who could make trouble, a man who looked after his money, a man who was not quite a gentleman.

The air hostess thought he was interesting. She guessed he was North Country, which he might have been, and rich, which he was not. She put his age at about fifty, which was about right. She guessed he was single, which was half true. Somewhere long ago there had been a divorce; somewhere there were children, now in their teens.

'If you want another whisky,' said the air hostess, 'you'd better hurry. We shall be at London Airport in twenty minutes.'

'No more.' He didn't look at her; he was looking out of the window at the grey-green fields of Kent.

(from *The Spy who Came in from the Cold* by John le Carré – adapted)

59

C When is your birthday?

1 Say these dates.

June 21, 1919 (*'June the twenty-first, nineteen nineteen'*)

May 8, 1986

July 17, 1600

December 12, 1945

October 3, 1844

March 11, 1911

2 Answer the questions.

1. What is the date today? ....

2. What day is it? ....

3. What is the time? (Answer in words, not figures.) ....

4. What day is tomorrow?...

5. What day was yesterday? ....

6. What day is your birthday this year? ....

7. If today is February 28, 1984, what is tomorrow's date? ....

8. If today is Friday, what is the day after tomorrow? What was the day before yesterday? ....

....

9. If the day before yesterday was Friday, is the day after tomorrow Tuesday? ....

....

3 Read this description of picture A. Then complete the description of picture B.

This is a picture of a small dark room. There are only three pieces of furniture: a chair, a table and a cupboard. There are two people in the room – a man and a woman. The man is standing by the window talking to the woman, who is sitting at the table.

This is a picture of a .... There are fourteen .... :
.... , and ....
There are .... in the room – a woman .... The
.... talking .... , who ....
....

4 Describe the room that you are in now.

D   Have you got a cat?

1 Write ten sentences.

I have got / I have not got

a   some   enough
too much   too many
a lot of   any

....

My boss   My brother
My girlfriend
My mother   My uncle
....

has got
has not got

a   some   enough
too much   too many
a lot of   any

....

2 Singular countable noun, plural countable noun or uncountable noun?

shirt   eye   hair   ear-rings   ears   jeans   wool   glasses   water   watch
apple   beer   snow   foot   bank   money   feet   pounds

SINGULAR COUNTABLE
shirt

PLURAL COUNTABLE
ear-rings

UNCOUNTABLE
hair

61

3 Which one is different? Why?

1. milk   tomato   steak   chair   wine   *chair — not food or drink* ....
2. milk   wine   water   whisky   apple   ....
3. chair   TV   fridge   bus   sofa   ....
4. chair   TV   fridge   sofa   armchair   ....
5. chicken   horse   cow   pig   sheep   ....
6. chicken   dog   cow   duck   sheep   ....
7. April   February   Thursday   September   ....
8. January   February   March   May   July   ....
9. Africa   America   Japan   Australia   Asia   ....

It's a long story PART 13

4 Read this with a dictionary.

Sam Watson was standing at the arrivals gate at Rio airport, holding a bunch of flowers. He was worried. Judy's plane was three hours late and nobody knew why. Sam walked over to the bar and had a drink. He walked back to the arrivals gate. No news. He walked back to the bar and had another drink. Still no news... Back to the bar...

Two hours (and eight drinks) later, Judy's plane landed, and after another half hour the passengers started coming out. Sam smiled, and looked for Judy. After a time he stopped smiling. Finally, the last passenger came through. It wasn't Judy. Sam said a big bad word. What had happened? He went over to the information desk. 'My name's Sam Watson,' he said. 'Have you got any messages for me?' 'Yes,' said the stewardess. 'A telephone message from Scotland.' She handed him a paper. 'Mr Sam Watson, Rio airport. Have a nice holiday. Don't come back. Love, Jasper MacDonald.' Sam said another big bad word, tore up the paper, and gave the flowers to the stewardess. 'What time's the next plane to London?'

Behind Sam, a tall beautiful girl was listening to his conversation. When she heard the word 'London', she smiled.

62

Ordering and asking

A I'll have roast beef

1 Change *not any* to *no*; change *no* to *not any*. Examples:

There isn't any beer. *There's (no) beer.*

I've got no friends. *I haven't got (any) friends.*

1. There are no more potatoes. Do you want me to buy some? ....

2. There isn't any petrol in the can. ....

3. I didn't spend any money yesterday. (I spent...) ....

4. Fifty million years ago there were no people. ....

5. There aren't any good films on TV this evening. ....

6. We haven't got any food in the house. ....

2 Put in *some more, any more, a little more* or *no more*.

1. 'Have you got *any more* cigarettes?' 'I'm sorry, I haven't.'

2. Let me give you .... coffee.

3. 'Is there .... fish?' 'Yes, here you are.'

4. I've got .... jazz records. Would you like to hear them?

5. There are .... mushrooms, but we've got some tomatoes.

6. 'Can you lend me £5?' 'I haven't got .... money – I gave it all to you yesterday.'

7. 'Would you like anything more to eat or drink?' 'Just .... tea, please.'

8. I'm very hungry. Could I possibly have .... potatoes?

3 Use your dictionary. Find out the names of these things and learn them.

....

....

4 These are extracts from diaries written by adolescent boys in London. The first time you read them, use a dictionary to look up the <u>underlined</u> words.

'I got up and had sausage, egg, bacon and tomatoes for breakfast and read the *Sunday Mirror*. Then my brother Wally knocked at the door. He asked me if I wanted to go fishing with him and June, my <u>sister-in-law</u>. I quickly got my boots on and went with them in their van. We got to Broxbourne at about 12.30 and Wally and me started fishing and June started getting the dinner with a <u>calor gas</u> cooker. We had sausage, egg and bacon again, after that a cup of hot orange and a piece of swiss roll. Then it started to rain. It poured down and we all got <u>soaked</u>, so we made for home. When we got back they came in and Mum made us a hot cup of tea. Then Wally and June went off home.'

'Today I got up at eight o'clock and went swimming with my uncle. We got to the York Hall baths at nine. There were not many people in there. We <u>fooled around</u> and had <u>a couple</u> of <u>races</u>; I lost both. We came out at 10.30 and I came home.'

'My cousin and I took the dog out for a walk at 10.15. We stayed out quite a long while looking for girls.'

'I had my tea, washed and left for the girl-friend's house. When I arrived her mother let me in and told me to take a seat in the living-room. We watched television for most of the evening.'

'8.30 p.m. My fiancée came round. We went to see my nan*, who lives in the same flats as me. We always have a good laugh when we go to see her, and my girl loves hearing her talk about the people she meets in the market every day.'

'About half past seven I went round my fiancée's flat, and sat down with her mum and dad and had a talk with them. We watched television for a while and then all went out for a drink.'

* *nan*: grandmother

(from *Adolescent Boys of East London* by Peter Wilmott)

Could you lend me some sugar?

1 Can you complete the following sentences *without looking at* the Student's Book?

1. '................... .... trouble

....

lend .... tea?'

'..................., of ....'

2. '................... me.

.... got .... light,

...................?' 'Just ....

...................'

3. 'Have ....

.... cigarette?' '...................,

.... don't ....'

4. '................... ....

.... dictionary?'

'................... afraid ....

.... got ....'

2 Match the rooms and the verbs.

1. kitchen   2. bedroom   3. bathroom   4. living room   5. dining room   6. garage

a. wash   b. sit and relax   c. keep a car   d. sleep   e. cook   f. eat

Example: ...*6 c*........

Now make sentences. Example: *You can keep a car in a garage.*...................

3 Fill in the table.

60 *seconds*.........	= 1 ....
60	= 1 ....
24	= 1 ....
7	= 1 ....
52	= 1 ....

4 Crossword puzzle.
Use a dictionary.

(Solution on page 128.)

ACROSS

1. Between hip and foot.
3. .... me, have you got a light?
7. I'm sorry, there's .... more roast beef.
9. Just a ....
12. Not wet.
13. You drive it.
14. You see with it.
15. My name .... George.
16. I'm sorry to .... you.
17. United Kingdom.

DOWN

1. Could you .... me your umbrella, please?
2. I .... to work by bus.
4. 'Could I borrow your dictionary?' 'Yes, of ....'
5. You usually do this at night.
6. Do you .... English?
8. Have you got any brothers .... sisters?
10. She's a very n..e person.
11. At the end of your finger.

C Something to drink?

1 Put in *who, what, how, where.*

1. '............ time is it?' 'Seven-thirty.'

2. '............ do you get to work?' 'By bus.'

3. Excuse me, ...'s the nearest post office?

4. .... colour are your baby's eyes?

5. .... old are you?

6. '............'s today?' 'Tuesday.'

7. '............ wrote *Symphonie Fantastique*?' 'Tchaikovsky?' 'No, Berlioz.'

8. .... much money have you got with you?

9. Excuse me, can you tell me .... I can buy cigarettes?

10. '............ long does it take to learn English?' 'Not very long.'

11. '............ far is it to the station?' 'About a mile.'

12. '............ are you?' 'Fine, thanks.'

2 How would you like to do or be these things?

I would love to   I would not like to
I would like to   I would hate to
I would quite like to

go to the moon.   live in the year 2500.   travel round the world.
know everything.   speak ten languages.   be a cat.   be a flower.
be Scottish.   be a film star.   be President of the world.

3 Match the words and the pictures.

something to eat
something to drink
something to play
something to wear
something to read
something to eat with
something to sit on
something to look at
something to listen to
something to live in

1. *Something to eat*

2. ....

3. ....

4. ....

5. ....

6. ....

7. ....

8. *something to sit on*

9. ....

10. ....

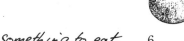

4 **Refuse these requests. Answer like this:**

I'm sorry. I'm afraid I | haven't got one.
| haven't got any.
| need it.
| need them.

1. Could I borrow your car this afternoon? ....

2. Excuse me, could you lend me an umbrella? ....

3. Could you give me some beer? ....

4. Could you possibly lend me your tennis shorts? ....

5. Have you got a dictionary that I could look at? ....

6. Excuse me, could you lend me a little sugar? ....

7. Could I borrow your guitar for half an hour? ....

5 **What did you do yesterday? Write about 100 words.**

D I like Alice; Alice likes me

1 Put in *I, me, my, you, your, he, him, his, she, her, it, its, we, us, our, they, them* or *their*.

1. Excuse ...., can you tell .... the time?

2. We'd like to see .... again. Can you give .... your address?

3. 'Is this .... bag?' 'Yes, it's mine. Could you put .... on the table, please?'

4. Your daughter looks like ....

5. Can you meet .... at the station? I'm arriving at 6.15.

6. 'Does John know there's a party?' 'Yes, I phoned .... this morning.'

7. There's a letter for Sally. Could you give it to ....?

8. His clothes don't fit ....

9. I can't remember where we parked .... car.

10. What time is ....?

11. 'Do you know Bruce and Daphne?' 'Yes, but I don't like .... much.'

12. We are going to see a film. Would you like to come with ....?

13. Children usually think that .... parents don't understand .... are usually right.

14. 'Can I help ....?' 'Yes, thanks.'

15. 'Is that .... dog?' 'Yes.' 'It's a friendly little thing. What's .... name?'

2 Complete this conversation.

A: .... some cake?

B: No, ... to eat, thanks, but I'd like ....

A: I'm sorry, I haven't got .... except ....

B: Water's OK, thanks.

3 Put in *something, anything, nothing* or *everything*.

1. I'd like .... to read, please.

2. I'm afraid there isn't .... to drink.

3. He's very intelligent. He knows .... about politics and economics.

4. The baby understands .... that you say to her.

5. 'Would you like a beer?' 'No, ... to drink, thank you.'

6. Please speak more slowly. I can't understand ....

7. Let's eat in a restaurant. There's .... in the house.

8. I've got .... in my eye. Could you look at it, please?

9. Is there .... to eat in the fridge?

4 Read this with a dictionary.

As the night plane took off, Sam closed his eyes. He loved travelling, but he was always a little afraid of flying. He couldn't really understand how the plane stayed up in the air. Also, he was worried about what would happen to him. Would there be detectives waiting for him at London airport? It was crazy to leave Brazil. In Brazil there was sun, freedom and beautiful women. He could live happily for years with his £50,000. In Britain there was rain, trouble, policemen and a strong chance of prison. But he had to see Judy. Judy was different. Judy was special. Sam smiled and opened his eyes. Next to him there was sitting a tall, incredibly beautiful girl. 'Hello,' said Sam. 'My name's Sam.' 'I know,' said the beautiful girl. 'My name's Detective Sergeant Honeybone.' Sam closed his eyes again.

It's a long story PART 14

18

The present

A What's happening?

1 What are you wearing now?

2 Say what some of these people are doing now (or what you think they are doing).

your mother   your father   your wife/husband/ boyfriend/girlfriend   your boss   your teacher your Prime Minister/President   one of your friends your children (if you have any)

3 Say what is happening in the picture below.

"And this comment from your music teacher — 'I hope your boy enjoys his holiday as much as I'm going to enjoy mine'…"

B The Swan-Walter Universal Holiday Postcard Machine

1 Write the *-ing* form.

speak *speaking*	play	drive
stop	run	shop
make	lie	smoke
work	fight	get
live	wear	go
		think

2 Complete these conversations.

A: Hello. Cardiff 345 5928.

B: Hello, Jenny. .... is Owen. .... Mike, please?

A: I'm sorry, he can't come to the phone just now, Owen. ....ing.

B: OK, I'll ring back later.

A: I'll tell .... you called. Bye.

B: Bye.

⎯⎯◇⎯⎯

A: What ....ing?

B: Chocolate. .... like some?

A: No, thanks. .... like chocolate.

3 Change the expressions as in the examples.

1. a man who has got a moustache *a man with a moustache*

2. a woman who has got long hair ....

3. a boy who is wearing blue jeans *a boy in blue jeans*

4. a girl who is wearing a striped skirt ....

5. a woman who is wearing glasses ....

6. somebody who has got a long nose ....

7. a man who has got brown eyes ....

8. a girl who is wearing a short skirt ....

4 What did you do last weekend? Write about 100 words.

C Things are changing

1 How are you changing?

(Are you getting fatter / thinner / taller / richer / poorer / better at English / more tired / happier / unhappier / more beautiful / more handsome / more intelligent / . . . ?)

Write some sentences beginning 'I am getting ...'

2 Complete the sentences with some of these words and expressions.

are getting	army	changing	is happening	price	height	average
problem	fast	unemployed	slowly	are going	worse	is getting

1. The .... of petrol is going up again.

2. Three years ago there were two million people without jobs. Now there are over three million ....

3. The housing problem is getting ....

4. Food prices .... up.

5. Things are changing very .... these days.

6. Restaurants .... more and more expensive.

7. In 1981, the .... cost of a good meal for two, with wine, was £25.

8. There are 300,000 men in the ....

9. What ....? I can't see.

3 Read this with a dictionary.

The population of Great Britain is increasing at about 0.66% per year. (World population is increasing at 2% per year – 220,000 a day – and will double in 35 years.) Life expectancy in Britain is also increasing: in 1840, men lived for an average of 40 years and women for 42; in 1970, the average life expectancy was 69 years for men and 75 for women. People are getting taller, too. A thirteen-year-old Glasgow boy was, on average, 13cm taller and 21kg heavier in 1966 than in 1910.

Religious belief is becoming less common. In 1920, 87% of British people said they believed in God; in 1973, the figure was 74%.

Even the weather is changing. In 1980, the average temperature in the Northern Hemisphere was 1.5°C lower than during the period 1940–5.

4 True or false? (The answers are in the text in Exercise 3.)

1. The British population is increasing very fast. ....

2. People live longer in Britain today than they did 100 years ago. ....

3. Men live longer than women. ....

4. Boys in Glasgow are not as tall as they were 70 years ago. ....

5. In 1920, most British people believed in God. ....

6. The weather is getting warmer. ....

D Grammar: the two present tenses

1 Put in the correct verb tense.

1. I would like to go home now. .... late. (It gets / It's getting)

2. 'What ....?' 'Beer. Can I give you some?' (do you drink / are you drinking)

3. 'Where's Lucy?' '............................ a bath.' (She has / She's having)

4. What sort of films ....? (do you like / are you liking)

5. 'Do you speak French?' 'No, ...' (I don't / I'm not)

6. What time .... to bed? (do you usually go / are you usually going)

7. Have you got anything to eat? .... hungry. (I get / I'm getting)

8. The Scots .... the best whisky in the world. (make / are making)

9. Italians .... more wine than English people. (drink / are drinking)

10. 'What ....?' 'I'm practising the guitar.' (do you do / are you doing)

2 Pronunciation. Say these sentences with the correct stress.

1. **What** are you **do**ing?
2. **What's** she **eat**ing?
3. **Where** are they **go**ing?
4. **What** did she **say**?
5. **How** do you **know**?
6. **Why** are you **drink**ing my **tea**?
7. **When** do you **want** to **come**?
8. **What time** are you **go**ing to **work** tomorrow?
9. **Who** did you **see** **yes**terday?
10. **What** are you **do**ing this **even**ing?

3 Look at the examples and then put the words in the right order.

1 2 3
Is your brother *working* today?

1 2 3
Does Mr Allison *play* the piano?

1 2 3
What *are* those people *drinking*?

1 2 3
Where *do* your parents *live*?

1. does Wagner work where Mrs ? ....

2. fast does like George cars ? ....

3. eating girl that what is ? ....

4. often boss how on holiday does your go ? ....
....

5. those are singing why men ? ....

6. Smith dinner to us are Mr coming with Mrs and ? ....
....

7. for does what wife breakfast have your ? ....
....

8. Dr working today is Harris ? ....

4 Read this with a dictionary.

When Judy woke up the next morning the sun was shining, the birds were singing, and everything was beautiful. Her room was lovely, and she felt fine. There was a knock on the door, and in walked the ghost, carrying a cup of tea. 'Did you sleep well?' he asked. 'Yes, beautifully,' said Judy. 'And thank you for a wonderful dinner last night.' The ghost blushed. 'Not at all,' he said. 'It was just a simple meal. I'm glad you enjoyed it.'

The evening before, after a magnificent dinner (cooked by the ghost), Judy and Jasper had talked far into the night – about life, love, art, death, music, books, travel, philosophy, religion, politics, economics, astronomy, biochemistry, archaeology, motor-racing and many other subjects. Most of all, they had talked about themselves. And when they had said goodnight, Jasper had kissed her, very gently. She could still feel the touch of his lips. What a perfect evening! Judy smiled at the memory. She stopped smiling. She had to go to Rio to see Sam. Sam was her boyfriend. She loved him. The sun went behind a cloud. The birds stopped singing. Judy started getting dressed as fast as she could.

Plans

A Who's doing what when?

1 Can you solve this problem?

Here are posters for next week's entertainments in the small Fantasian town of South Lyne. Unfortunately, extremists have painted out all foreign names (Fantasian surnames always end in -*sk*). The four missing names are: James O'Connor, Maurice Ducarme, Richard Haas and Antonio Carlotti.

– Haas isn't musical.
– O'Connor is leaving Fantasia on the morning of the 22nd.
– Ducarme is a famous actor.

Who is doing what when?

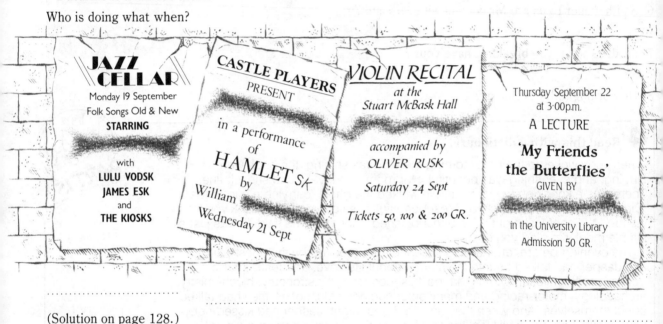

JAZZ CELLAR
Monday 19 September
Folk Songs Old & New
STARRING

with
LULU VODSK
JAMES ESK
and
THE KIOSKS

CASTLE PLAYERS
PRESENT

in a performance
of
HAMLET SK
by
William
Wednesday 21 Sept

VIOLIN RECITAL
at the
Stuart McBask Hall

accompanied by
OLIVER RUSK

Saturday 24 Sept

Tickets 50, 100 & 200 GR.

Thursday September 22
at 3·00p.m.
A LECTURE

'My Friends
the Butterflies'
GIVEN BY

in the University Library
Admission 50 GR.

(Solution on page 128.)

2 What are you doing tomorrow? (Write 50–100 words.)

3 Put in *and, but, or* or *so.*

1. It's a nice day, ... it's cold.

2. What would you like to drink – beer .... wine?

3. We've got five children – three girls .... two boys.

4. I'm very tired, ... I think I'll go to bed.

5. Until three years ago I smoked twenty cigarettes a day,
   .... the doctor told me it was bad for me, ... I stopped.

6. I like Annie and Fred, ... I don't like their mother (who
   lives with them), ... I don't often go to see them.

7. Have you got any animals – a cat .... a dog, ... anything?

4 Complete the conversation.

PAT: Hello, Waterford 31868.

BILL: ....?

PAT: Speaking.

BILL: Oh, hello, Pat. It's Bill. ....?

PAT: No, I'm sorry, I'm not.

BILL: ....?

PAT: My uncle's coming to dinner with us.

BILL: Well, are you free on Thursday?

PAT: ....

BILL: ....?

PAT: I'd love to. What time?

BILL: Let's meet at eight at ....

PAT: OK.

BILL: ....

B We're leaving on Monday

1

How soon is your birthday? – in a few weeks? – in three months? .... How soon is Christmas? .... How soon is your next English lesson? .... Next Tuesday? .... The year 2000? .... Your next holiday?

....

2 Put in *at, on, in, for* or no preposition.

1. Are you free .... Friday evening?

2. Come round to my place .... about nine o'clock tomorrow.

3. I'm going to California .... Christmas .... two weeks.

4. We usually go and stay with Amanda and Stephen .... August.

5. The pub's closing .... five minutes. Would you like another drink?

6. Let's go and see Christine .... tomorrow night.

7. Can I talk to you .... a few minutes?

8. 'Are you busy?' 'Yes, but I'm going to be free .... about an hour.'

"How about Thursday night, then?"

3 Imagine that you are going on a journey round the world, starting next Monday. Write about your schedule. For example:

On Monday I'm flying to New York. I'm staying in New York for three or four days; then I'm hiring a car and driving to Los Angeles. Then ....

73

4 Revision crossword.

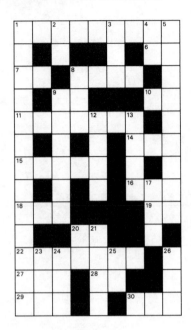

ACROSS

1. Everest, Mont Blanc, Ben Nevis.
6. You and I.
7. How .... you ....?
8. Can I .... you?
9. That man.
10. ....'s six o'clock.
11. Edinburgh is a .... centre in Scotland.
14. John's nice. I like ....
15. 'Are you Carol Williams?' 'Yes, that's ....'
16. Mary's a shop assistant. .... starts work at 8.30.
18. Have you got .... sweaters in my size?
19. 'What colour?' 'Either blue .... red.'
20. The same as *19 across*.
22. It goes on your ear.
27. Dinosaurs lived millions of years ....
28. The opposite of *yes*.
29. The opposite of *old*.
30. You can open a ....

DOWN

1. A sea.
2. I get .... at nine o'clock on Sundays.
3. My mother, father, brothers and sisters are .... fair-haired.
4. North-west.
5. Month.
8. She's nice. I like ....
9. I'm terribly .... Have you got anything to eat?
12. The opposite of *out of*.
13. 'How much is that ring?' '............ one?' 'No, the other one.'
17. '............ do you get to work?' 'By bicycle.'
20. The same as *20 across*.
21. It goes on your finger.
23. 'What's your ....?' 'Twenty-seven.'
24. You can do it in a small boat.
25. The same as *28 across*.
26. $(6 + 6) \times 6 - 6 \div 6 + \frac{6}{6} - 6$.

(Solution on page 128.)

Let's go to Scotland

1 Complete these conversations.

A: Excuse me. Do you know where I can buy a colour film?

B: ....

A: Thanks anyway.

———◇———

A: ....

.... ?

B: At the supermarket.

A: .... ?

B: First right, second left.

A: .... ?

B: About two hundred yards.

A: ....

B: Not at all.

Sally: ....

Bruce: Hello. Could I speak to Lorna, please?

Sally: ....

Can I take a message?

Bruce: No, it's all right. I'll ring back later.

Sally: OK. ....

Bruce: ....

———◇———

A: .... go to the cinema tonight.

B: No, let's .... theatre.

A: No, I don't want ....

B: OK. Why .... go and see Mother?

A: No. Look, ... don't we stay .... home and .... TV?

B: Good idea. OK.

2 Put in the right preposition.

1. We're leaving here .... three days.

2. I had a drink with Peter .... Tuesday.

3. I usually work .... nine o'clock .... five.

4. This is a picture of my family .... holiday.

5. We spent three weeks .... the mountains.

6. I'm getting up .... six o'clock tomorrow.

7. I'm driving .... Scotland.

8. I'm staying with friends in Edinburgh .... four days.

9. I don't like travelling .... train.

10. 'Can you help me?' 'Yes, ... course.'

3 Read this with a dictionary.

A DREAM

Last night I had a strange dream. I was in a world where all the colours were different. The grass was orange, the trees were white; in the green sky there was a purple sun and a moon the colour of blood. I was a child again, eight years old, and I was lost. I felt very frightened and unhappy. In front of me there was a long street, stretching away as far as I could see. There were no people, but all around me I heard the noise of big insects. It was terribly hot. Suddenly a door opened on my left. I went into the house and ran up the stairs. When I got to the top, I saw a field full of blue horses. I called one of them; he came over to me and I got on his back. I don't know how far he took me – we went through forests, across rivers, past high mountains covered with black snow. At last we came to a town. The streets were full of people dressed in red. Nobody spoke. I said goodbye to my horse and walked until I came to a church. Inside I heard my mother's voice. I pushed the door, but it was too big and heavy – I couldn't move it. I called as loud as I could, but nothing happened. Then, very slowly, the door opened. In the church there were hundreds of people, all looking at me. They started to come towards me, slowly at first, then faster and faster... Then I woke up.

D Meet me at eight

1 Pronunciation. Say the sentences with the correct stress.

What are you **do**ing this **eve**ning?
Would you **like** to **come** to the **c**inema **with** me?
How about to**mor**row?
We're **lea**ving on **Mon**day.

Just for **two days**.
Back on **Fri**day **night**.
The **child**ren are **go**ing to **Mo**ther.

2 Complete the story with these words.

got into	kissed	understand	when	saw	woke up
then	suddenly	didn't	sing	that	difficult	road
along	smiled	because	drive	fast	night	couldn't

A DREAM

Last .... I dreamt .... I was in a very .... car,

driving .... a road in Ireland. It was raining, and I ....

see very well. Then .... I .... a woman standing in the

middle of the .... I stopped, she .... the

car and told me to .... to Dublin. It was .... to

.... her, ... she had a strange accent. She started to

..............., and .... she looked at me and smiled. I asked her

name, but she .... answer. She .... again, and

.... me on the cheek. Then I ....

3 Write the story of a dream. (About 100 words.) Use some of these words and expressions. (Look at page 75 to see how they are used.)

I had a strange dream	I felt very frightened	in front of me	all around me
suddenly	I saw	there was	he came over to me	nothing happened
very slowly	faster and faster	I woke up	

4 Read this with a dictionary.

When Sam woke up he felt terrible. He had a headache, and there was a horrible taste in his mouth. He looked out of the window. The sun was shining, and through a gap in the clouds he could see the sea. It was a long way down. Sam shivered and turned to look at Detective Sergeant Honeybone. She looked fresh and lovely – even more beautiful than the evening before. 'Good morning,' she said. 'Did you sleep well?' 'No,' said Sam. 'Excuse me.' He got up and walked forward to the toilets.

　　After a wash and a shave, Sam felt a little better. He brushed his hair, put his jacket back on, and looked at his tongue in the mirror. Not a pretty sight. Sam put his tongue back in, took out his gun, and looked at his watch. Time to move. He came out of the toilet, glanced round quickly, and then walked to the front of the plane. Opening the door of the cockpit, he stepped inside. 'This is a hijack,' he said. 'Take me to Loch Ness.' 'Oh, God,' said the pilot. 'Not again. What's so special about Loch Ness?' 'Jasper MacDonald,' said Sam.

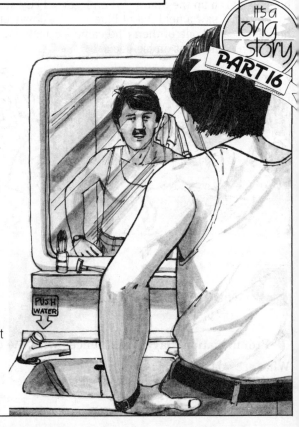

Getting to know you

A Is this seat free?

1 Complete the conversations.

A: .... seat ....?

B: No, ... it ....

———◇———

A: .... car?

B: Sorry, ... need ....

———◇———

A: .... mind .... look at .... newspaper?

B: .... all.

———◇———

A: .... borrow .... pen?

B: .... course.

2 Some of these words are pronounced with the vowel /i:/, like <u>eat</u>. Some of them are pronounced with /ɪ/, like <u>it</u>. Some are pronounced with neither /i:/ nor /ɪ/. Say the words, and then write them in three groups according to the pronunciation.

please live five give green pol<u>i</u>ce d<u>i</u>nner friend sing s<u>i</u>ster ski this these fine people him
jeans bread <u>E</u>ngland b<u>ui</u>lding pr<u>e</u>tty steak g<u>ui</u>tar fridge meat meet feel speak cheap

GROUP 1 (like *eat*)	GROUP 2 (like *it*)	GROUP 3 (other)
please	live	five
green	give	friend
police	dinner	

3 Read this text; if necessary, look up the <u>underlined</u> words in a dictionary. (The writer is talking about a time during the Second World War, when he was hiding from the Germans in an Italian hospital.)

Then the *superiora*, the head of the <u>hospital</u>, appeared, a middle-aged woman with a gentle, resolute face. She was carrying a large <u>tray</u> loaded with tea things and bread and butter, ginger biscuits and raspberry jam. I tried to thank her, partly in French, partly with the few Italian words I knew, but they got mixed up with bits of school Latin, and then I ran out of words completely and looked at her in despair, and she smiled and went out of the room and came back with the girl I had met in the farmyard that morning.

She was wearing a white, open-necked shirt and a blue cotton skirt. She was brown, she was slim, she had good legs, she had ash blonde hair and blue eyes and she had a fine nose. When she <u>smiled</u> she looked <u>saucy</u>, and when she didn't she looked <u>serious</u>. She was all right.

'You have not forgotten me?' she said. I assured her that I had not done so.

'My mother has made an *apfelstrudel* for you,' she said. 'In my country we call them

77

struklji. We are not Italian. We are Slovenes. You can eat it after your dinner. Tonight you have chicken. The *superiora* told me. Be kind to her and do what she says. Now I must go. I have to take food to your friends.'

I asked her when she would come again.

'I will come tomorrow, if the *superiora* allows. If you want I will teach you Italian. It will be <u>useful</u> for you, and you can teach me English. I speak badly. My name is Wanda.'

(from *Love and War in the Apennines* by Eric Newby – adapted)

 Do you often come here?

1 Put in *always, usually, very often, often, quite often, sometimes, occasionally, hardly ever, never.*

1. It .... rains in Britain.

2. People .... get up late on Sundays.

3. Women .... win the Nobel prize.

4. Good-looking people .... have nice personalities.

5. Policemen .... smile.

6. Politicians .... tell the truth.

7. Women .... give flowers to men.

8. Elephants .... eat meat.

9. Passport photographs .... look like the people.

10. Prices .... go up.

11. People .... live to be 100 years old.

12. Holidays .... cost too much money.

2 How often do you:

go to the theatre?   travel by bus?   dance?   drink wine?   play tennis?   go swimming?
go to church?   listen to the radio?   write letters?   drive a car?

Examples: *I travel by bus twice a day. I play tennis every Saturday.*

3 Write 'reply questions' to answer the following sentences. ('*Are you?*' '*Is it?*' etc.)

1. I work on Saturday mornings. ....

2. The plane leaves at 10.45. ....

3. I like swimming. ....

4. Andrew eats like a horse. ....

5. My father's got a flat in North London. ....

6. I've got a new car. ....

7. Robert came to see us yesterday. ....

8. Your sister looks like you. ....

9. You're very beautiful. ....

4 Say these sentences, and then put them in groups according to the rhythm.

Where are you from?   John's a nice man.   There were two cars.   How do you do?
Buy a large steak.   Do you live here?   First on the left.   Not the green one.   English and French.
In a red car.   Do you like fish?   Thirty-five days.   What do you want?

Group 1   Group 2   Group 3

□□□□   □□□□   ?

Where are you from?   *John's a nice man.*   ....

How do you do?   ....

....

....

....

C What do you think of...?

1 What (or who) is your favourite song/sport/country/town/drink/food/painter/composer/season/
writer? (Write at least five sentences.)
Example: *My favourite sport is cycling.*

2 Answer these questions.

1. Do you like horses? ....

2. What do you think of golf? ....

3. Do you like poetry? ....

4. Do you like Western films? ....

5. Do you like cats? ....

6. What do you think of the government? ....

7. Do you like driving fast? ....

8. What do you think of pop music? ....

9. Do you like Mozart? ....

10. Do you like English? ....

Possible answers:
(Yes,) I like it/them very much.
(No,) I don't like it/them much.
I quite like it/them.
I don't think much of it/them.
I think it is / they are interesting/
boring.

3 Complete the sentences.

1. My mother likes skiing, and so .... I.

2. All my friends can dance, but I ....

3. 'I've got a new dress.' 'That's funny, so ....'

4. 'I'm Capricorn.' 'So ....'

5. 'I'm tired.' '...................... not.'

6. 'My brother can speak six languages.' 'So .... I.'

7. 'Where do you live?' 'Oxford.' 'That's funny. So .... I.'

8. 'I like smoked salmon.' 'Oh, I .... at all.'

4 Do you know?

1. What is the capital of the USA? ....
2. What is the capital of Northern Ireland? ....
3. How many inches are there in a foot? ....
4. What does EEC mean? ....
5. Are there pyramids in Mexico? ....
6. Where is the Sphinx? ....
7. Where do elephants live? ....
8. Name two German cars. ....
9. How many kilometres are there in five miles? ....
10. What was the old name of Leningrad? ....
11. What does a polar bear do when it meets a penguin? ....
12. How many cents are there in an American quarter? ....

(Answers on page 128.)

 D I've only known her for twenty-four hours, but...

1 Put in the 'past participles' and learn the irregular verbs.

INFINITIVE	PAST	PAST PARTICIPLE
live	lived	*lived*
work	worked	*worked*
start	started	....
stop	stopped	....
play	played	....
change	changed	....
be	was	*been*
know	knew	....
have	had	....
see	saw	....
read (/ri:d/)	read (/red/)	....
write	wrote	....
hear (/hɪə(r)/)	heard (/hɜːd/)	....

2 Complete the sentences with past participles.

1. Have you ever .... *Carmen?*
2. How long have you .... married?
3. How long have you .... my friend Andrew?
4. How long have you .... that car?
5. Have you ever .... to Scotland?
6. Have you ever .... any of Agatha Christie's detective stories?
7. Have you ever .... Beethoven's first symphony?
8. Have you ever .... a poem? (write)

3 Put in the correct verb form.

1. Where .... you ....? (live)
2. How long .... you .... there? (live)
3. .... you .... my friend Alison Haynes? (know)
4. How long .... you .... her? (know)
5. How long .... you .... that watch? (have)
6. .... you .... today's newspaper? (read)
7. .... you .... Mary today? (see)
8. What .... you .... of your new boss? (think)
9. How long .... you .... learning English? (be)
10. Why .... you learning English? (be)

"Have you been waiting long, Sir?"

4 Read this with a dictionary.

It's a long story PART 17

Judy ran downstairs and into the dining room. No Jasper – only the ghost. 'Can I help you?' he asked politely. 'Would you like some breakfast?' 'Where's Jasper?' asked Judy. 'He's gone out,' said the ghost. 'Oh, dear,' said Judy. 'Lend me a pen and paper, could you?'

Quickly she wrote a note to Jasper:
'Dear Jasper,
      It was wonderful. But I have to go. I'm sorry. I wanted to say goodbye to you, but perhaps it is better like this.
      Thank you for a beautiful memory.
      Judy.'

She said goodbye to the ghost, who looked sad, and walked out of the castle. Not far along the road there was a bus stop. If she could get to Inverness before lunch, she could catch the afternoon plane to London and buy some new clothes before catching the night flight to Rio. Tomorrow morning she could be in Sam's arms. How wonderful! Judy started crying.

At the bus stop, Judy read the timetable. Buses for Inverness ran every three hours, but she was lucky – there was one in twenty minutes. As she stood waiting, she looked out over the lake. A few hundred yards away there was a man fishing in a boat. She could hear him singing in the clear still air. He had a wonderful voice – a voice that Judy recognized – and he was singing an old Scottish love song. It was Jasper. Tears came into Judy's eyes, and she looked away from the boat, up into the peaceful sky. High above Loch Ness, a golden eagle was flying in circles. There were pretty little clouds looking like splashes of white paint against the deep blue. And two parachutes.

Things

A Why...? Because...

1 Match the nouns and the adjectives.

disco music   a diamond
helium   lightning   a whale
lead   a mouse   Superman
a tortoise   an atom   butter
the Amazon   the Bering Strait
a Californian redwood tree

hard   soft   strong
loud   quiet   big
small   wide   narrow
tall   light   heavy
fast   slow

2 Put in *that, because, when, if, where, and,* or *but*.

1. Elephants can't jump .... they're too heavy.

2. Do you mind .... I open the window?

3. I'm sure .... Maria can't speak French.

4. Can you tell me .... I can buy petrol?

5. She looks stupid .... actually she's very intelligent.

6. I'm very hungry, ... I didn't have any breakfast this morning.

7. I always visit John and Barbara .... I go to London.

8. Henry can play the guitar .... he can sing quite well too.

3 Put in *a, an* or *the* where necessary; or don't put anything.

John Calloway is ...*a*.... bank manager. He works in ...*a*.... bank in ..*the*... centre of ...—.... London. Every morning he gets up at seven o'clock, has .... breakfast and .... cup of .... coffee, and reads .... *Times*. Then he goes to .... work by .... bus. In .... morning he usually makes .... telephone calls, sees .... customers and dictates .... letters. He has .... lunch at .... restaurant near .... bank. In .... afternoon he works until five or five-thirty, and then goes .... home. He doesn't work on .... Saturdays or .... Sundays: he goes to .... cinema or reads. He likes .... novels and .... history. He is not married. He has .... sister in .... Oxford and .... brother in .... London.

B What's a car made of?

1 Can you see:

something made of wood, something made of metal, something made of plastic, something made of rubber, something made of paper, something made of stone, something made of glass?

Find their names in a dictionary and write them down. Example:

made of wood: a door, the floor

2 Look at this example.

a book

Is it animal, vegetable or mineral?   Is it living?   Is it useful?

It's vegetable and mineral.   *No, it isn't.*   *It depends on the book.*

Now answer these questions.

a leather handbag

Is it animal, vegetable or mineral? ....

Is it living? ....

Can you eat it? ....

Is it made of wool? ....

Is it useful? ....

Can you find it in a kitchen? ....

Is it liquid? ....

Is it very heavy? ....

Is it soft? ....

Is it manufactured? ....

Have you got one of these? ....

Can you see one now? ....

Does everybody have one? ....

Can you put things in it? ....

Is it made of plastic? ....

Can you open and close it? ....

3 Read enough of this to give a letter to each picture. You can use a dictionary.

If silica is melted and allowed to cool slowly, the result is glass. Glass is more difficult to make than pottery, and the first all-glass containers did not appear until 1500 BC. Glass was made then by (A) melting raw silica held by a glass thread on a sand core to form a bottle or (B) shaping it in a mould. It was not until 1350 BC that the technique of blowing glass was developed. A wine glass was made (C) by blowing melted glass in a mould, adding a stem, shaping the foot and trimming. Press moulding (D) is an even more modern technique. Glass-working tools (E) include a blowpipe, rod, tongs, shears and rolling plate. Glass was originally melted in a crucible (F); later bell (G) and cone (H) furnaces were used.

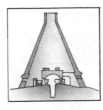
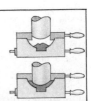

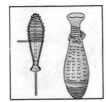
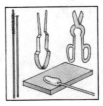
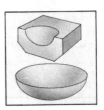

C 'The best car in the world'

1 Choose two of these three tasks (A and B, or B and C, or A and C). You can use a dictionary.

A. Read this and compare some of the figures (numbers) with a car you know.

HOW THE ROLLS-ROYCE SILVER SPIRIT PERFORMS

TEST CONDITIONS:
Wind: 10-15 mph
Temperature: 22 deg C (67 deg F)
Barometer: 29.6in Hg (1005mbar)
Humidity: 60 per cent
Surface: dry asphalt and concrete
Test distance: 2,072 miles

FUEL CONSUMPTION

Overall mpg: 14.0 (20.2 litres/100km)
3.08 mpl.

Constant speed:

mph	mpg	mpl	mph	mpg	mpl
30	20.2	4.43	70	16.2	3.56
40	20.2	4.43	80	14.6	3.21
50	19.0	4.18	90	12.8	2.81
60	17.6	3.87	100	10.6	2.32

OIL CONSUMPTION

(SAE 10W/30) 1,000 miles/litre

ACCELERATION

FROM REST

True mph	Time (sec)	Speedo mph
30	3.3	31
40	5.1	41
50	7.3	51
60	10.0	62
70	13.4	73
80	17.6	84
90	23.2	96
100	30.8	109
110	43.5	121

Standing ¼-mile: 17.1 sec, 79 mph
Standing km: 31.9 sec, 101 mph

IN EACH GEAR

mph	Top	2nd	1st
0-20	–	–	2.6
10-30	–	–	2.2
20-40	–	3.4	3.1
30-50	–	4.2	–
40-60	6.3	5.8	–
50-70	7.8	6.7	–
60-80	9.1	–	–
70-90	10.4	–	–
80-100	13.2	–	–
90-100	20.3	–	–

MAXIMUM SPEEDS

Gear	mph	kph	rpm
Top (Mean)	119	192	4,540
(Best)	119	192	4,540
2nd	74	119	4,240
1st	40	64	3,820

PRICES

Basic	£41,830.00
Special Car Tax	£3,485.83
VAT	£6,697.37
Total (in GB)	**£52,113.20**
Seat belts	Standard
Licence	£70.00
Delivery charge (London)	£70.00
Number plates	£18.00
Total on the Road (exc. insurance)	**£52,227.12**

(speedo = speedometer   mph = miles per hour   mpg = miles per gallon   mpl = miles per litre)

B. Use the text to put the pictures in order.

ANGRY MOTORIST 'KILLS' CAR

Bellevue, Washington (UPI) –
A driver became angry Tuesday when his car got stuck in the snow, broke its windows with a tyre iron, and then took out a pistol and shot the tyres, police said.

'He killed it,' said police Major Jack Kellem.

The car got stuck in 6 inches of snow.

Police said the driver became so angry that he took a tyre iron from the boot and broke all the windows in the car. Still not satisfied, he took out a pistol and shot holes in all four tyres.

When the pistol jammed, he threw it into the snow and returned to the tyre iron.

When police arrived, he was beating on the bonnet.

Major Kellem said the man had not been drinking.

The driver was jailed for shooting a pistol in the city.

C. The pictures are in order. Find the correct order for the text.

BOY DRIVER SAVES FATHER

a. Mr Spencer is doing well in hospital, and doctors say Mark did the right thing.

b. But he didn't stop to call an ambulance; he pushed his father across the seat and drove to the nearest hospital.

c. Nine-year-old Mark Spencer was out for a drive with his father.

d. Mark is only four feet tall: he can just see over the dashboard and reach the pedals with his feet.

e. He drove two miles on a busy road. 'I did drive through a red light once, but there weren't too many problems,' said young Mark.

f. Then 47-year-old Philip Spencer had a heart attack, and stopped the car just in time.

g. His mother, Blanche Spencer, says, 'Thank God he was with his father and not me: I can't drive.'

2 EITHER: cut out a picture of a car from a magazine and write the names of some of the parts on it (you can use a dictionary)
OR: write a few sentences about a kind of car that you like.

D Where was your car made?

1 These sentences are not true. Correct them.

1. The sun goes round the earth.

   The sun does not go round the earth.

   OR *The earth goes round the sun.*

2. It never rains in Scotland. ....

3. Britain exports rice. ....

4. Spain imports oranges. ....

5. Mice eat cats. ....

6. The British drive on the right. ....

7. Brazilians speak Spanish. ....

8. Wood is heavier than lead. ....

9. The Atlantic is as big as the Pacific. ....

10. The Nile is as long as the Amazon. ....

11. Spaghetti is grown in Norway. ....

12. A pound of rice is heavier than a pound of gold. ....

2 Try the crossword puzzle.

ACROSS

3. Opposite of *quiet*.
5. 'Why can't you come to the party?'
'........... it's my best friend's birthday, and I'm taking him to dinner.'
6. His sister's .... architect.
7. Do you .... if I smoke?
8. I've been to America ....: once in 1982 and once last year.

10. Judy and I live in the same street, so we drive to work ....
12. Did you .... to Barry's yesterday?
13. I've known her .... twelve years now.
15. I'm .... the doctor about my leg tomorrow.
17. Opposite of *heavy*.
18. It's a quarter .... four.
19. Do you mind .... I call you Mike?
20. Be careful! I .... my finger on that knife yesterday.
21. How long .... did you start working here?
22. Opposite of *high*.
25. I'm seeing her .... Tuesday.
26. Could I .... your pen for a minute?

DOWN

1. 'Where's John, do you know?' '........... was here a minute ago.'
2. I didn't sleep well last night – the bed in the hotel was too ....
3. Some shoes are made of ....
4. Could you speak a little louder? I can't hear you – they're .... and playing loud music upstairs.
7. Keys are made of ....
9. 'Where's the front door key?' 'I left .... on the table.'
11. Is the room warm .... for you?
14. Her family has been in the village .... 1726.
15. It's very late – is Bernard .... at the office?
16. It's .... colder: I think it will snow tonight.
17. The new car is .... than the old one, so it's more difficult to park.
23. '........... didn't Janice come?' 'I don't think she was invited.'
24. Debbie wasn't home, ... I left a message with her daughter.

(Solution on page 128.)

3 Learn these irregular verbs.

INFINITIVE	PAST	PAST PARTICIPLE
make	made	made
cost	cost	cost
go	went	gone

INFINITIVE	PAST	PAST PARTICIPLE
eat	ate	eaten
drink	drank	drunk
come	came	come

4 Read this with a dictionary.

Sam and Detective Sergeant Honeybone hit the water together. Sam went under and came up. 'Help!' he shouted, going under again. 'I can't swim!' he shouted, as he came up again and went under for the third time. Sam's life passed in front of his eyes as he went down, down, down into the green water. His childhood in London. Visiting his mother and father in prison. His first girlfriend. His first bank robbery. Judy. Judy. He would never see her again.

'Don't worry, you lovely man,' called Detective Sergeant Honeybone. 'I'm an Olympic 400-metre gold medallist.' She swam over to him with beautiful strong strokes, caught him under the arms as he came up again, and started pulling him towards the boat.

'Hello, Isabel,' said Jasper as they pulled Sam out of the water. 'What are you doing here? And why have you got Sam with you? He's the last person I want to see.' 'It's a long story,' said Detective Sergeant Honeybone. 'I'll tell you later. Wait while I give Sam the kiss of life.' 'I don't need the kiss of life,' said Sam. 'Oh yes you do,' said Detective Sergeant Honeybone.

THERE IS NO PRACTICE BOOK WORK FOR UNIT 22.

Instructions

A How to do it

1 Fast reading. Read these instructions fast but carefully, and do exactly what they say. Time-limit: two minutes.

Write your surname on a piece of paper. Don't write your first name. If it is Tuesday, write your age, but if it is Thursday, write the date. If it is neither Tuesday nor Thursday, don't write anything, but draw a circle round your name. Write the name of your country, in English, under your name. If you have not already written the date, write it to the left of the name of your country. If you are over thirty, do not write the name of an animal, but if you are thirty or under, write the name of an animal and the name of a bird at the bottom of the page.

2 Read the text and put the pictures in the right order.

Exercise Ten   Run and hop

Start Stand erect, feet together, arms at sides. Starting with left leg, run in place raising feet at least four inches from floor. (When running in place lift knees forward, do not merely kick heels backwards.)

Count Each time left foot touches floor counts one. After each fifty counts do ten hops.

Hops Hopping is done so that both feet leave floor together. Try to hop at least four inches off floor each time.

(from *Physical Fitness*)

A

B

C

Answer: ....

3 Here are some instructions about how to drive a car. Put *always, never* or *don't* before each one. Use a dictionary.

1. .... look in the mirror before driving off.

2. .... drive fast in fog.

3. .... drive too close to the car in front.

4. .... forget to check the oil from time to time.

5. .... wear your seat belt.

6. .... put a small child in the front seat.

7. .... drive on the right in Britain.

8. .... overtake when you can't see a long way in front.

9. .... drive at over 30 miles an hour in towns.

10. .... park on a double yellow line – it can be expensive.

B Be careful!

1 Put the words with the right notices. Use a dictionary.

ⓑ PLEASE DO NOT FEED THE ANIMALS

ⓓ NO PARKING

ⓔ **Please Check Your Change**

ⓐ **DO NOT DISTURB**

ⓒ **NO SMOKING**

Please shut ⓕ the gate

ⓖ **Please Take One**

ⓗ **DO NOT WALK ON THE GRASS**

Answers: 1. .... 2. .... 3. .... 4. .... 5. .... 6. .... 7. .... 8. ....

2 Write some notices for your school.

3 Put one of these expressions in each blank.

| look out | come in | look | don't worry | wait here |
| follow me | be careful | please hurry | take your time |

1. *Be careful* .... – there are eggs in that box.

2. .... Everything's all right.

3. .... and sit down, Mr Pearson. What can I do for you?

4. .... My plane is at four o'clock, and it's 3.15 now.

5. ...., please. Your seats are right over here.

6. ....! There's your brother over there!

7. ....! There's a car coming!

8. Ms Wilsdon is busy at the moment. Could you ...., please?

9. 'I'm terribly sorry.' 'That's all right. I'm not in a hurry. ....'

4 Try this crossword.

A C R O S S

1. £ $ DM   ¥
6. .... are pineapples grown?
8. The opposite of *cheap*.
10. I can run faster .... my brother.
12. A lot of wheat is .... in the USA.
13. Sweaters made from lambs' wool are ....
14. Opposite of *good*.
18. It .... me an hour to drive to work.
19. I can't drink this coffee – it's .... hot.
21. The opposite of *hot*.
22. My car was too .... for the narrow road.
23. Mountains are ....
24. He can't walk home; it's .... too far.

25. Me, ..., her, him, us, them.
26. The opposite of *2 down*.
28. Their children are ....; the oldest is three.
31. It weighs 0.5 grams – it's very ....
32. John is taller than his brother, but they both weigh the same: John's ....
33. Cars are made of ....

D O W N

1. This car was .... in Sweden.
2. You can't talk in my car – it's too ....
3. Britain and Germany .... coffee from Brazil.
4. I always wear comfortable clothing .... I run.
5. Where .... pineapples grown?
7. Germany and France .... cars to the USA.
9. A Volkswagen is more .... than a Rolls-Royce.
10. I don't think .... her brother can drive.
11. He's not .... tall .... his wife.
15. My daughter is fair now, but I think that she'll be .... when she's older.
16. I can't phone him .... I haven't got his number.
17. People are in this room about one third of their time.
20. The shop is .... from nine to five.
22. '...........?' 'Because.'
26. She's .... tall, but not as tall as I am.
27. How far is it .... the nearest phone box?
29. The same as *31 across*.
30. I don't like opera; rock music is much .... interesting.

(Solution on page 128.)

89

C On and off

1 Write instructions to change picture A to picture B. Example:

..... Take the jacket out of the room. .....

2 Match the sentences and the replies.

1. 'I'm hungry.'   a. 'Why don't you hurry?'
2. 'I'm thirsty.'   b. 'Would you like a sandwich?'
3. 'I'm tired.'   c. 'Why don't you go to bed?'
4. 'I'm bored.'   d. 'There's a good film on TV.'
5. 'I'm unhappy.'   e. 'Can I do anything to help?'
6. 'I'm late.'   f. 'Have a drink.'

3 Read the text and put in the missing words and expressions.

a moment	across	against	and	at	behind
by	don't	good	his	in	into	looking at	of
on	picked up	put	slowly	standing	throw
up	want	was			

'.......................... move. Nobody move.' The

voice .... calm, slow

.... deadly. 'Now

.... your guns ....

the middle .... the room.
Everybody. That's right. Put your hands

.... and get back

.... the wall, nice and slow. Keep
your hands up, lady. That's very

.... Now turn round

.... and face the wall. And if you

.... to stay alive, just keep looking

.... that wall. You too, Mr Galvin.'

.... him, Galvin heard a key turn

.... the door of the safe. He moved

his head a little, ... the reflection

in .... glasses. The big man was

.... with his back to them

.... the safe, looking inside. With
one smooth movement, Galvin turned and dived

.... the table; ....

later, the big man was lying .... the

floor gasping for breath. Galvin ....

his gun and .... it in his pocket.

'Tell them to send a younger man next time,' he
said.

(from *A Gun for your Money* by Neil MacShaw)

4 What did you do yesterday evening?

D **Recipes**

1 Read the recipe and fill in the blanks. You can use a dictionary.

MUSHROOMS FRIED WITH ONION
..................: about 20 mins.

.... *(to serve 4)*
¾ .... *large mushrooms*
1 large onion
3-4 .... salad oil
Salt, ...
Parsley

Utensils
Large frying-pan
Knife
Chopping knife and
*   board*
.... cloth

1. Wash the mushrooms, but .... not peel. Cut .... most of stalk. Pat .... gently.

2. Peel and .... onion fairly fine.

3. Heat salad .... in pan – not too hot. Put in ...., stalk side up, ... fry gently .... 10 mins.

4. Chop parsley.

5. Turn mushrooms, ... onion, and .... another five .... or a little more.

6. .... on hot dish, sprinkled with ...., pepper, and parsley.

2 Write instructions about how to boil an egg.

3 Learn these irregular verbs.

INFINITIVE	PAST	PAST PARTICIPLE
throw	threw	thrown
put	put	put
get	got	got
leave	left	left
do	did	done
sleep	slept	slept

4 Read this with a dictionary.

It's a long story PART 19

'All right,' said Jasper. 'I suppose we'd better go back to the castle and find you some dry clothes. Pity. I was hoping for a quiet morning's fishing.' He rowed the boat over to the bank of the loch and they got out. Detective Sergeant Honeybone picked up Sam in her beautiful strong arms and they started walking down the road towards the castle. As they passed the bus stop, Jasper walked over to Judy, who was staring up at the sky. 'Good morning, you beautiful creature,' he said. 'Going shopping? Don't forget lunch is at 12.30.' Judy turned her back, tears streaming down her face. 'Don't talk to me about lunch,' she said. 'I'm going to Rio to see Sam.' 'But Sam's here,' said Jasper. 'Don't try to talk me out of it,' said Judy. 'I've made up my mind, and I…what did you say?' She turned round and looked across the road. There was Detective Sergeant Honeybone, standing with a soft smile on her lips looking down at Sam, who was lying in her arms with his eyes closed. Judy's mouth fell open.

Getting around

A A room for two nights

14 Nights from £439

NEW YORK & LOS ANGELES

A week in New York and a week in Los Angeles – Two vastly contrasting cities each with its own magic appeal.

New York, New York – It's a wonderful town! The Statue of Liberty, Empire State Building, World Trade Centre, Broadway, shops galore. Spend a whole week exploring the fabulous 'Big Apple'.

California, here we come! – glamorous Los Angeles, Hollywood, Capital of the film and record industry, Disneyland, Universal Studios, the Beaches of Malibu and Santa Monica. Plenty to do and see in Sunny Southern California.

Fly into New York's John F. Kennedy Airport and upon arrival our Jetsave representative will arrange your transfer to the Century Paramount Hotel, situated just off Broadway, which will be your home for the first 7 nights. During your first week you will have plenty of opportunity to see the sights of

this fascinating city. Why not book a day trip to Atlantic City, the Las Vegas of the east?

California bound, you board a United Airlines Jumbo flight to Los Angeles where your accommodation has been reserved at the Hollywood Roosevelt Hotel on Hollywood Boulevard. Your Jetsave representative will be on hand to assist with your sightseeing. Don't go home without saying 'Hi!' to Mickey Mouse in Disneyland. Take an overnight tour to the entertainment capital of the world – Las Vegas – it's all there for you.

1 Use the text to answer these questions.

1. The 'Big Apple' is a name for ....

2. What part of California is Malibu in? ....

3. Who will help you get from the airport to your hotel? ....

4. Which airline flies Jetsave travellers from New York to Los Angeles? ....

5. Disneyland is near ....

6. Atlantic City is near ....

7. Las Vegas is fairly near ....

2 Complete the conversation. Try to do it without looking at the lesson in the Student's Book.

RECEPTIONIST: ....?

TRAVELLER: .... double room, ...

RECEPTIONIST: .... night?

TRAVELLER: ....

RECEPTIONIST: ....?

TRAVELLER: Shower, please.

.... ?

RECEPTIONIST: £18 ....

TRAVELLER: Including ....?

RECEPTIONIST: Yes.

TRAVELLER: .... cheque?

RECEPTIONIST: Yes, if you have a cheque card.

.... register, ...?

TRAVELLER: ....

RECEPTIONIST: Your .... 403.

TRAVELLER: ....

3 Can you divide?

£54 for three nights = £18 a night. £6 for three kilos = £2 a kilo.

300 kilometres in three hours = ...

600 words in ten minutes = ...

£5 for ten hours = ...

100 miles in ten days = ...

30 lessons in ten weeks = ...

21 meals in a week = ...

 You have to change twice

1 Put in words and expressions from the lesson.

1. Piccadilly Circus is .... from Green Park to Leicester Square.

2. You can .... from Oxford Circus to Paddington .... changing.

3. If you go from Notting Hill Gate to Green Park you .... change.

4. Marble Arch is .... as Bank.

5. If you go .... South Kensington ...., where do you ....?

6. 'How far is it to Victoria?' 'It's the next ....'

2 Answer the questions. Use *by bus, by train, by underground, by bicycle, by motorbike, by car, by air,* or *on foot.*

1. How do you get from your home to your school?..

2. How do you travel to work? ....

3. How do you travel when you go on holiday? ....

4. How do you get to the cinema? ....

5. How do you go from your home to the bank? ....

6. How do you get from your home to the station?..

7. How do you get from your home to the nearest airport? ....

8. How do you travel to the nearest foreign country? ....

93

3 Read the text with a dictionary. Then write a few sentences about public transport in your country.

LONDON TRANSPORT

Public transport in London is expensive. The fare depends on the length of the journey; you cannot buy books of tickets in advance. Children under 16 pay half, and those under five travel free. You usually buy bus tickets from a conductor, but on some buses you pay the driver. Most London buses are 'double-deckers'; you can smoke upstairs. On the underground railway ('tube') you buy your ticket from a machine or a ticket office, and give it up at the end of the journey. Not all trains from one platform go to the same place, so watch the signs. The last train leaves at about 00.15.

C Flight 3 to Hong Kong

1 Put in *they're*, *their* or *there*.

1. .... late.

2. .... flight from Bergen is delayed.

3. What are they doing ....?

4. .... travelling from Naples.

5. .... isn't a direct flight.

6. .... baggage is in Madrid.

2 These are the answers to questions about the timetable. Make the questions. Example:

Twice a week. *How often does Flight BA11 go via Muscat?* ....

1. Four times a week. ....

2. On Thursdays. ....

3. Only on Mondays. ....

4. At 0605. ....

5. At 19.45. ....

6. By 16.30. ....

7. QF018. ....

8. Yes. ....

9. No. ....

LONDON—BRISBANE 747
DEPART London, Heathrow Airport. Terminal 3 (Minimum check-in time 60 mins; BA First & Club class 45 mins)
ARRIVE Brisbane International Airport

Frequency	Aircraft Dep	Arr	Via	Transfer Times	Flight	Aircraft	Class & Catering
Mo	1945	0945‡	Muscat, Singapore, B Seri Begawan, Sydney		BA11	747	FCM ✗
We	2045	0945‡	Muscat, Kuala Lumpur, Singapore, Sydney		BA11	747	FCM ✗
Th	1730	0605‡	Athens, Bahrain, Singapore, Darwin		QF018	747	FY
Sa	2045	0945‡	Abu Dhabi, Kuala Lumpur, Singapore, Sydney		BA11	747	FCM ✗

‡ —Two days later

"Doesn't it make you sick? Our baggage has been sent to Jupiter."

3 Read the text; you can use a dictionary.
Then answer the questions. Put one or more words in each blank.

THIEFROW

Thefts at London's Heathrow airport have been put as high as £5 million a year. Here are some examples:

1. A hitchhiker, dressed in an airline anorak, stopped a British Airways van at the airport in 1973. He said he wanted a lift to another part of the airport. Once in the van he pulled out a pistol and escaped with its cargo – diamonds from a Ghana Airways flight and platinum from South African Airways, just arrived from Johannesburg. His haul was worth £467,000.

2. The simplest crime netted the thief £2 million. He was working for an air courier firm. One summer day he went round the firm's clients, picking up the packets of money and valuables due to be sent by them. He then got on a plane and flew to Switzerland with the £2 million. His previous criminal record had not prevented his employment as a courier of banknotes; but the flashy behaviour that had tipped off police on his earlier crimes was soon noticed by the Swiss police.

(from *Airport International* by Brian Moynahan – adapted)

1. The driver of the van thought the thief worked for ...., because he was ....
   Perhaps the thief chose the van because he .... the cargo was ....

2. A courier is a person who travels with .... and .... for other people.
   The thief was .... before he became a courier.
   The thief probably didn't use his own name when he went to ...., because the British police .... his name and could find him by looking at the list of ....

Walk along the river bank...

1 Which one is different?

1. low   tough   (understand)   soft
2. more useful   better   higher   narrow
3. boarding pass   factory   reservation   check-in
4. interesting   heavy   high   wide

5. grapes   calculators   cameras   cars
6. metal   radio   glass   plastic
7. saw   woke   took   been
8. platform   return   door   single
9. double   region   single   bath

2 Put the verb in the correct tense.

1. I ...*saw*... Adrian yesterday. (see)

2. What .... you .... later this evening? (do)

3. Why don't you take an umbrella – I think it .... (rain)

4. .... you ever .... at the restaurant next to the station? (eat)

5. I usually .... to work by bus, but last Tuesday I .... on foot. (come)

6. Do you mind if I .... the window? (open)

7. I'm sorry, Katy can't come to the phone – she .... a bath. (have)

8. I .... Joanne for three years, but I can't say I always .... what she's thinking. (know)

3 Imagine an English friend is coming to visit you in your home. Write a letter, giving precise instructions on how to drive to your home from the main road into your city/town/village.

4 Learn these irregular verbs.

INFINITIVE	PAST	PAST PARTICIPLE
pay	paid	paid
say	said (/sed/)	said (/sed/)
buy	bought	bought
sell	sold	sold
speak	spoke	spoken
wake	woke	woken
break	broke	broken

It's a long story PART 20

5 Read this with a dictionary.

JUDY: Who is that woman?
JASPER: May I introduce my sister Isabel? Isabel, this is Judy.
SAM: If you're Jasper's sister, why is your name Honeybone?
ISABEL: It's a long story. Give me a kiss, Sam.
JUDY: Put that man down at once.
JASPER: Ladies, ...
ISABEL: Who is that woman, and why is she wearing my sweater?
JUDY: Sam, get down.
ISABEL: He's not feeling very strong.
JUDY: That's all right. I'm a medical student. I'll look after him.
ISABEL: Oh, no. You're not playing doctors with my Sam.

JASPER: Ladies, ...
JUDY: He's not your Sam. He's my Sam.
ISABEL: Take my sweater off at once.
JASPER: Ladies, please.
JUDY: / ISABEL: Shut up.
JUDY: Sam, protect me from this mad woman.
ISABEL: It's all right, Sam. Don't pay any attention to her. I'll look after you.
JASPER: Sam, where are you going?
JUDY: / ISABEL: Sam, come back!
(splash!)

Knowing about the future

A This is going to be my room

1 What are you going to do this evening? Tomorrow? Next weekend? Write at least eight sentences.

2 Say these sentences with the correct stress.
1. **What** are you **going** to **do**?
2. I'm **not** going to **have** a holiday **this year**.
3. I'm **never** going to **speak** to you **again**.
4. **Who's** going to **clean** the **car**?
5. **What film** are you **going** to **see**?

3 Choose the correct tense.

1. I .... Lucy since Friday. (haven't seen / didn't see)

2. My mother .... Mrs Carpenter better than I do. (knows / has known)

3. She .... her for years. (knows / has known)

4. How long .... English? (have you been learning / are you learning)

5. What .... this evening? (are you doing / do you do)

6. .... to Australia? (Have you ever been / Did you ever go)

4 1. Read the first text.
2. Complete the second text with words and expressions from the first text.
3. Write about the plans of somebody you know who is going to study.

ANDY'S PLANS

Andy has just left school.
Next year he is going to
travel. He says 'I want to get
some experience of life
before I start studying.' He is
going to spend six months in
South America and six
months in the Far East. First
of all he is going to get a job
in a factory in Brasilia – his father has got business
contacts there. When he goes to the Far East he is
going to try to find work teaching English.

    After his year abroad Andy is going to study
engineering at St Andrews University in Scotland.

RUTH'S PLANS

Ruth ....
to leave school next summer.

She ....

to .... engineering at
Brunel University,

.... London, but
before going there she wants

to .... a year working. She says

'................ ....

some work experience ....

....' She is ....

.... spend six months in Italy and six

.... in Britain, working in car ....

where her teacher has got ....

B It's going to rain

1 Look at each picture, and say what is going to happen.

1. ....

2. ....

3. ....

4. ....

5. ....

6. ....

7. ....

2 What is going to happen in the next hour? Write down as many things as you can think of.

3 Pronunciation. Say these sentences.

Where are you going to **live**? **When** are you going to **pay**?
Who are you going to **see**? **Why** are you going to **do** it?
My **par**ents are going to **move** to **Lon**don.
The **chil**dren are going to **leave school**.
Prices are going to **go up**.

4 Make sentences with *is going to* or *are going to*.

1. What time | you | be home tonight? *What time are you going to be home tonight?*
2. When | your parents | move to London? ....
3. Why | your daughter | study engineering? ....
4. How | we all | travel to Scotland? ....
5. Where | Alice | buy her new car? ....
6. Who | cook supper? ....

C Why? To...

1 Tourists go to Switzerland to climb the mountains, or to ski, or to enjoy the scenery. They go t the USA to see New York, or to visit the West, or to practise speaking English. Write ten sentence to say why tourists go to France, or to Britain, or to India, or to Japan, or to other countries.

2 Make sentences.

Women put on make-up   People write letters
People go to casinos   People study languages
People travel   People go to pubs
People study philosophy

to win money.   to get better jobs.
to see the world.   to look more beautiful.
to get answers.   to learn useful and important thing
to pass the time.   to...

3 Read the words of the song with a dictionary.

I KNOW AN OLD LADY

I know an old lady who swallowed a fly.
I know an old lady who swallowed a fly.
I don't know why she swallowed a fly.
Perhaps she'll die.

I know an old lady who swallowed a spider
that wriggled and jiggled and tickled inside her.
She swallowed the spider to catch the fly,
but I don't know why she swallowed the fly.
Perhaps she'll die.

I know an old lady who swallowed a bird.
Now how absurd, to swallow a bird.
She swallowed the bird to catch the spider
that wriggled and jiggled and tickled inside her.
She swallowed the spider to catch the fly,
but I don't know why she swallowed the fly.
Perhaps she'll die.

I know an old lady who swallowed a cat.
Now fancy that, to swallow a cat!
She swallowed the cat to catch the bird,
she swallowed the bird to catch the spider...

I know an old lady who swallowed a dog.
What a hog, to swallow a dog!
She swallowed the dog to catch the cat,
She swallowed the cat to catch the bird, ...

I know an old lady who swallowed a goat.
She just opened her throat and swallowed a goat.
She swallowed the goat to catch the dog,
She swallowed the dog to catch the cat, ...

I know an old lady who swallowed a cow.
I don't know how she swallowed a cow.
She swallowed the cow to catch the goat,
She swallowed the goat to catch the dog, ...

I know an old lady who swallowed a horse.
She's dead, of course.

(© Southern Music Publishing Company Ltd.)

4 Try the crossword puzzle.

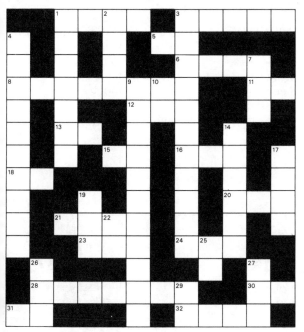

 1. She didn't cry much when she was a ....
3. The Mississippi is one.
5. You and I.
6. Can you .... on your way home and get some eggs?
8. I've got a lot of ideas, but I'd like to .... them a bit more before I talk to you.
11. 'Where's Janet?' '............ the butcher's.'
12. Neither Jack .... Terry could answer the question.
13. Did you .... to your Spanish lesson yesterday?
15. I have .... finish this work by five o'clock.
16. Are you going by ...., or are you taking your car?
18. My mother-in-law usually comes to dinner .... Fridays.
20. How .... you get here?
21. You can't go to the USSR without a ....
23. I am .... going to be there.
24. Same as *23 across*.
28. You find planes here.
30. I was born .... New Year's Day.
31. I'd like to pay .... cheque.
32. I don't know what's happening – I can't see .... the top of the wall.

DOWN
1. Have you got any hand ....?
2. She's .... here since nine o'clock this morning.
3. I've got my ticket, but I haven't made a .... for the return journey yet.
4. There should be traffic lights at that ....!
7. 'How are you going to ....?' 'In cash.'
9. I'd like some .... about flights to Majorca.
10. Rosa's English isn't very good, ... we all spoke Spanish.
14. I paid for the petrol by .... card.
17. If you come from the station, our house is on the left .... of the street.
19. I played cards with her all evening, and I didn't .... once.
22. She wasn't there, ... I left a message.
25. I can take you to the station – it's .... my way home.
26. How much did you .... for your car?
27. Come and see what I've bought – this is .... my mother, and this is .... Debbie.
29. What's the best way to get .... Charing Cross from here?

(Solution on page 128.)

D To and -ing

1 Put in the infinitive (with or without *to*) or the *-ing* form.

1. I very much like .... (swim)
2. How do you .... *sayōnara* in English? (say)
3. Can you .... me £5? (lend)
4. I'm sorry .... you, but I need help. (trouble)
5. Maria Rosa's not much good at .... languages. (learn)
6. Shall we .... on holiday in August this year? (go)
7. 'Have another drink.' 'Sorry, I must ....' (go)
8. Thank you for .... me. (help)
9. Tomorrow will .... sunny. (be)

99

2 Stress.

1. **Say these words (they are all stressed on the first syllable).**

   breakfast **re**gister **num**ber
   dictionary **rail**way **air**port **plat**form
   office **pass**port **bag**gage **sen**tence

2. **Now say these words (they are all stressed on the second syllable).**

   in**clu**ding with**out** ex**pen**sive
   de**pends** up**stairs** ar**ri**val de**par**ture
   in**fin**itive

3. **And these (they are both stressed on the third syllable).**

   conver**sa**tion reser**va**tion

3 Learn these irregular verbs.

INFINITIVE	PAST	PAST PARTICIPLE
win	won	won
find	found	found
mean	meant	meant
meet	met	met
tell	told	told
think	thought	thought

4 Read this with a dictionary.

'North-east Highlands Police Control, calling all cars. Calling all cars. The hijackers of the Boeing 707 from Rio are believed to be in the Loch Ness area after leaving the plane by parachute about 20 minutes ago. Proceed at once to the vicinity of Castle Clandonald and begin searching.
Description as follows:
Man, British, medium height, dark hair, small moustache, small brown eyes, wearing a blue suit and black shoes. He is believed to be Sam Watson, who is wanted in connection with a series of bank robberies. He is carrying a gun, and may be dangerous. Woman, nationality unknown, tall, blonde, blue eyes, attractive, athletic build, wearing dark clothes and shoes. Nothing is known about her identity.
Approach these people with caution. Repeat, approach with caution.'

It's a long story PART 21

Feelings

A I feel ill

1 Complete the conversations.

A: I've got a cold.

B: ....?

A: How are you?

B: .... ill.

A: ....?

A: I've got ....

B: ....

A: What's the problem?

B: ....

A: Why don't you go to bed?

B: ....

A: .... temperature

B: I don't think so.

100

2 Write two or three sentences to say how you feel just now.

3 Put one of these words in each blank.

I	you	he	she	it	we	they
me	you	him	her	it	us	them
my	your	his	her	its	our	their

1. My brothers and I all look like .... mother.

2. Tell the children to bring .... favourite toys.

3. Mum's gone to bed – .... says .... is tired.

4. Did you write to Jim or talk to .... on the phone?

5. Could you show . ... that ring, please?

6. Don't worry about me and the children – .... will eat along the way somewhere.

7. I really like Don and Susan – .... are so easy to be with.

8. You can borrow .... map if you haven't got one.

9. Tell .... what the problem is and we will try to help you with it.

10. My brother lent me .... car last weekend.

4 The pictures are in order but the text is not. Match the parts of the text to the pictures.

 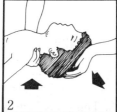 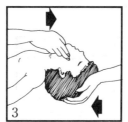 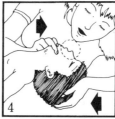 

a. Breathe into the child, but not too strongly. (A small child's lungs cannot hold your entire breath.) Take your lips away and let the child's chest go down while you take your next breath. Use fairly quick, short breaths, and keep it up until the child can breathe by himself or until help comes, as long as two hours.

b. Open the air passages by pulling the neck up and putting the head down very far.

c. If the child has got water in his lungs, first get it out by putting him on his stomach for ten seconds with his hips a foot higher than his head (over your knee, on a box, etc.).

d. Keep the child's chin pushed up all the time, to keep the air passages open.

e. With a child's small face you can breathe into nose and mouth together.

(from *Baby and Child Care* by Dr Benjamin Spock – adapted)

It frightens me

1 Underline the stressed syllables and say the sentences.

1. It makes me angry.
2. What's the matter? (2 stresses)
3. Would you like to have dinner with us tonight? (4 stresses)
4. There's nothing good on television. (3 stresses)
5. See you at seven o'clock. (3 stresses)
6. I can't understand my English lesson. (4 stresses)
7. I've got a headache. (2 stresses)
8. Why don't you take an aspirin? (3 stresses)

HOLY TRINITY ORTHODOX
SEMINARY LIBRARY

2 How do you feel about these?

1
2
3
4
5
6
7
8

Example:

7. *I think it's exciting.*

1. ....
2. ....
3. ....
4. ....
5. ....
6. ....
7. ....
8. ....

3 Complete the table. Then put the correct form of the verb in each sentence.

frighten	*frightens*	*frightening*	*frightened*
depress			
worry			
interest			
bore			
disgust			
excite			
tire			

1. Being a secretary is a very .... job. (tire)

2. My mother is .... because she has not heard from my sister for a month. (worry)

3. What a .... idea! (depress)

4. My Uncle Joe .... me to tears, but he's a kind old man. (bore)

5. Are you .... in old trains? (interest)

6. The present government .... my dad, but he does not want to vote for the other party. (disgust)

7. Mike's been asked to go to China. Isn't that ....? (excite)

8. I think Mark was ....; he fell asleep. (bore)

9. Sandra's school work is a bit .... – she did much better last year. (worry)

10. My son cooked dinner for us yesterday.

    It looked ...., but it tasted fine. (disgust)

11. Walking .... my mother now that she's older. (tire)

12. The children are very........................ about the holiday. (excite)

13. This book is very .... Could I borrow it for a week or two? (interest)

14. Edna is a very .... person to talk to. (interest)

15. Short December days .... me. (depress)

16. Sorry, I can't go out tonight, I'm too .... (tire)

17. Sheila was very .... after her boyfriend left, but I think she's much happier now. (depress)

18. Hamish .... about everything! (worry)

19. I think he left because he was .... with Jonathan's lying. (disgust)

20. The idea .... me, but I'm not sure I'll have time to do the job. (excite)

4 Complete the conversations.

A: How do you feel ………… bullfighting?

B: ………………………………………………… .

A: How do you ………………… flying?

B: ………………………………………………… .

A: I'm depressed.

B: ……………………………………… matter?

A: ………………………………………………… .

B: ……………………………… come to the cinema

……………… ?

A: That's ……………………………………………… .

C Do you like your boss?

1 Put the words in the right order.

1. for to work easy she's ………………………………………………………………………………

2. very talk he's to to difficult ……………………………………………………………………

3. work he's with nice to …………………………………………………………………………

4. with live to easy she's ……………………………………………………………………………

5. music pleasant listen this is to to ……………………………………………………………

6. with get to on easy she's ………………………………………………………………………

2 Use words from the lesson.

1. My mother …………… too much about details.

2. She's a …………… person.

3. We …………… problems together.

4. I'm a very patient person; I don't often …………… angry.

5. My boss gives me …………… work …………… I can do.

6. He …………… angry for stupid reasons sometimes.

7. …………… makes me angry when people …………… their minds again and again.

8. I like vodka, but I can't …………… whisky.

9. My girlfriend's easy …………… to.

10. My boss is difficult …………… work …………… .

3 Read what the young woman said in Exercise 4 in the Student's Book. Only use your dictionary to look up the underlined words.

Um, I work part-time in a pub, and my boss is obviously a landlord. Um, he's... smashing. He's got a great sense of humour, um, very easy to get on with, um, and is very fair. Um, he's... basically taught me the trade, because I was new when he, when I first came and he'd only just come to that pub as well, and he taught me, you know, everything that I needed to know, and wasn't, wasn't unfair when I made mistakes, and was very good to me, and, uh, smashing guy.

4 Write about somebody you know well; use a lot of words and expressions from the lesson.

OR: Imagine you live with a famous person. Write about how you get on with the person.

D Love at first sight

1 You don't know these words. How do you pronounce them? (Don't use a dictionary.)

tope   dune   slot   cope   dram   glide
slid   pride   hack   cube   grid   grate

2 Say these words with the correct stress.

under**stand**   pro**nounce**   re**mem**ber   for**get**   in**vite**
pre**fer**   in**clu**ded   ex**am**ine   pre**scrip**tion   to**mor**row
de**pressed**   dis**gust**   **morn**ing   **head**ache
aspirin (/ˈæsprɪn/)   **prob**lem   **med**icine (/ˈmedsən/)
pleasant   **marr**iage   ap**prec**iate   **terr**ible   ex**cit**ing

3 Put the past tense form of one of these verbs in each blank.

bring hear come put know lose tell say see
begin take(twice) make go can have wakeup

1. When I .... yesterday it was raining.

2. I .... Janet at the disco last night.

3. John .... Peter Sellers when he was a boy.

4. I .... some grape juice for you.

5. We .... the children to the Science Museum last week.

6. He .... his jacket on the bed, I think.

7. He .... he .... a headache, but I think he just didn't want to come.

8. How many people .... to the meeting last night?

9. When she was younger she .... run much faster than that.

10. They .... to Bali for two weeks in September.

11. Who .... you they were here?

12. I .... some people in the street at midnight last night.

13. I .... studying English when I was twelve.

14. I .... a terrible mistake yesterday.

15. She .... her sister with her.

16. Karen .... her glasses when she was in Spain.

4 Learn these irregular verbs.

INFINITIVE	PAST	PAST PARTICIPLE
take	took	taken
wear	wore	worn
run	ran	run
become	became	become
hurt	hurt	hurt
sing	sang	sung

It's a long story PART 22

5 Read this with a dictionary.

When Jock McHaverty was a little boy, he always wanted to be a bus driver. His father hoped he would go into the family business, and his mother would have liked him to be a doctor. But Jock just wasn't interested. He loved buses – all kinds of buses. He loved the way they looked, the smell of the diesel fuel, and most of all, the wonderful noise they made. When he was fourteen, he went on his first real holiday – a bus trip to the south of England and back. And when he left school two years later, he went straight into the Highland Bus Company.

Now Jock was one of the Company's most experienced drivers, working on the Fort William–Inverness route. This morning was fairly typical: he had eight passengers on board, and would probably pick up one or two more on the way. They were about twenty minutes late (Jock had stopped for a cup of tea and a chat at Strathnahuilish post office), but it didn't matter. 'Late' was not a word of any great importance in the Scottish Highlands. Jock leaned forward a little in his seat and smiled. It was a lovely day. The sun was shining on the loch, and the bus was running beautifully. Jock changed gear as they started up the long hill towards Clandonald Castle.

Movement and action

A How to get from A to B

1 Put in the correct preposition.

1. I went .... my sister's wedding yesterday.

2. 'Where did you first meet your wife?' '............ a party.'

3. Let's go .... a restaurant for lunch.

4. No, I don't like eating .... restaurants.

5. Mary's .... hospital. Shall we go and see her?

6. 'Come and have a drink.' 'Sorry, I can't. I'm going .... my guitar lesson.'

7. I got terribly cold .... the football match.

2 Write about some journeys that you have made, and say when you made them. Example:

In 1979 I went to Italy with my family. Last summer we drove to the mountains and camped there for six weeks. In April I cycled from my home to a friend's house, 50 kilometres away.

3 Read this with a dictionary.

RECORDS

When Apollo X was coming back to earth, it reached a speed of 24,791 miles per hour (39,897 kph) – the fastest speed at which men have ever travelled.

In 1977, a New Zealander ran 5,110 miles (8,224km) in under 107 days.

In 1979, an American ran 50 metres in 18.4 seconds on his hands.

Also in 1979, a New Zealander ran 100 yards (91.7m) backwards in 13.1 seconds.

In 1978, a blind English runner ran 100m in 11.4 seconds.

In 1931-2, an American walked backwards from California to Turkey.

The 24-hour record for walking backwards is 80.5 miles (129.55km).

The record for 1 mile (1.6km) on snowshoes is 6 minutes 23.8 seconds.

A man with one leg jumped 2.04 metres in 1981.

A man swam 1,826 miles (2,938km) down the Mississippi in 1930.

The record for non-stop balancing on one foot is 33 hours.

The non-stop crawling record is 26.5 miles (42.64km).

Another 1981 record: 13 Japanese cyclists rode one bicycle at the same time.

A Russian fell 6,700m (21,980ft) from a plane without a parachute in January 1942, and lived. A British flier jumped from a burning plane without a parachute in 1944, fell 5,500m (18,000ft), landed in a tree and a snowdrift, and was not hurt.

Some more records: dropping eggs without breaking them 650ft (198m); throwing eggs without breaking them 96.9m; non-stop guitar playing 230hrs; non-stop talking 159hrs; making a suit 1hr 34min 33.42 sec from sheep to finished suit (Australia 1982).

(from *Guinness Book of Answers*)

B Like lightning

1 Put in *who, how, what, where, when, why* or *which*.

1. '............ did you get here?' 'By train.'

2. .... is the nearest telephone?

3. '........... are you late?' 'Because I missed my train.'

4. .... tall are you?

5. .... wrote *War and Peace*?

6. .... are you thinking about?

7. .... is your birthday?

8. I don't know .... to pronounce 'apophthegm'.

9. .... platform for the London train?

2 Solve this problem as fast as you can.

Jane talks faster than Mary, who talks more slowly than George. Andrew talks faster than Jane, but not as fast as Alice, who talks faster than George, who (as you know) talks faster than Mary, who doesn't talk as fast as Jane.

Who talks fastest? ....

(Solution on page 128.)

3 Read this with a dictionary.

There is an old story, by the Greek philosopher Zeno, about a race between Achilles and a tortoise. Achilles could run very fast, while a tortoise, as everybody knows, is an extremely slow animal. In fact, Achilles could run ten times as fast as the tortoise. So Achilles gave the tortoise some help: he let him start ten metres ahead. If you look at the diagram, you can see the situation before the race started: Achilles is at A, and the tortoise at B. They have to race 100 metres.

Achilles

The tortoise

10 Metres

A   B

As soon as he heard the gun, Achilles started sprinting at top speed. The tortoise started sprinting too, but not quite so fast. Very soon, Achilles had reached B, the tortoise's starting point. But of course, the tortoise wasn't there any more; he had got to C.

A   B   C

'I'll catch him in no time,' thought Achilles, and ran on to C. But unfortunately, by this time the tortoise had reached D. And when Achilles got to D, the tortoise was already at E. Now E was not very far from D – only a centimetre – and Achilles got there very fast indeed. But now the tortoise was at F... And so it went on, through G and H and I, and the rest of the alphabet, and on past the end of the alphabet, for ever. So, although Achilles could run ten times as fast as the tortoise, he never caught him.
Moral: Never let the tortoise start first.

C If you press button A,...

1 Choose words to complete these sentences. Try to do the exercise first before looking at the list of words.

1. I was .... in London, ... June 16th, 1942, ... three

   o'clock .... the morning. I was a beautiful ....

2. I had a very strange .... last night. I was in a big red Rolls-Royce. We were going .... Dublin, and we were .... very fast, in the dark, without .... Suddenly I .... a white horse in the road .... front .... us. Then I ....

3. Who .... the film *The Third Man?*

4. I'd like to .... faster .... sound.

5. Light .... at 300,000km .... second.

6. 'What did she want?' 'I don't know. She .... so quietly that I couldn't .... what she said.'

7. What's that noise in the street? Look .... the window and see what's ....

8. She says she's 34, but .... she's at least 40.

9. The car went very well. We .... from Rome to Zürich at an .... speed of 65mph.

10. 'What's the world .... for the long ....?' '8m 90.'

directed	average	lights	baby	born	actually	spoke	woke up	dream	jump	travels	hear
out of	saw	driving	drove	happening	record	than	per	fly	on	at	to	in (twice)	of

2 Say where you got some of your possessions. Examples:

I got my sweater in London. I got my watch in New York. I got my ring from my mother. I got my shirt at Marks and Spencer's.

3 Say these sentences with the correct rhythm.

What are they **do**ing? **Where** are you **go**ing? **What** do you **think**? **When** can I **come**? **How** do you **know**? **Who** did you **see**? **Why** do you **ask**? **What** does she **want**? **When** did they ar**rive**? **How** can I **help**?

4 Fast reading. Read the text and find the answers to the questions as fast as you can. Time-limit: two minutes.

1. What is the record speed for a tennis serve? ....

2. What is the record average speed for 24-hour cycling? ....

3. What is the official land speed record? ....

4. What is the water skiing record speed? ....

5. What is the record speed for a one-hour walk? ....

SPEED IN SPORT

mph	km/h	Record	mph	km/h	Record
622.287	1001,473	Highest land speed (four wheeled rocket powered) (Official land speed record)	43.14	69,40	Track cycling (200 m 219 yd) unpaced in 10·369 s
			41.72	67,14	Greyhound racing (410 yd 374 m straight 26·13 s)
429.311	690,909	Highest land speed (wheel driven)	41.50	66,78	Sailing – 60 ft 18,29 m proa Crossbow II (36·04 kts)
319.627	514,39	Official water speed record	35.06	56,42	Horse racing – The Derby (1 mile 885 yd 2,41 km)
318.866	513,165	Highest speed motor cycle	27.00	43,5	Sprinting (during 100 yd 91 m)
250.958	403,878	Motor racing – closed circuit	25.78	41,48	Roller Skating (400 yd 402 m in 34.9 s)
188	302,5	Pelota	21.49	34,58	Cycling – average maintained over 24 hr
170	273	Golf ball	13.46	21,67	Rowing (2000 m 2187 yd)
163.6	263	Lawn Tennis – serve	12.26	19,74	Marathon run (26 miles 385 yd 42,195 km)
140.5	226,1	Cycling, motor paced	9.39	15,121	Walking – 1 hr
128.16	206,25	Water Skiing	5.28	8,50	Swimming (50 yd) – short course in 19·36 s
124.412	200,222	Downhill Schuss (Alpine Skiing)	4.53	7,29	Swimming (100 m) – long course in 49·36 s
63.894	102,828	Downhill Alpine Skiing (Olympic course) (average)			
52.57	84,60	Speedway (4 laps of 430 yd 393 m)			
43.26	69,62	Horse racing (440 yd 402 m in 20·8 s)			(from *Guinness Book of Answers* – abridged)

107

D Please speak more slowly

1 Put in the past tenses of the verbs.

1. I .... your mother yesterday. She's looking fine. (see)

2. You .... a letter from Sylvia this morning, didn't you? (get)

3. Who .... St Paul's Cathedral? (build)

4. I .... ill yesterday, so I .... to see the doctor. (feel; go)

5. It .... very late when I .... home last night. (be; come)

6. Alex .... a new car last week. (buy)

7. A man once .... 6,700m without a parachute, and lived. (fall)

8. My boss .... to New York again last week. (fly)

2 Make adverbs from these adjectives.

tired *tiredly* .... easy .... last .... sensitive ....

possible .... probable .... certain .... definite ....

hopeful .... cool .... quick .... heavy ....

3 Write about a journey you once made. Use as many words and expressions from Unit 27 as you can. Write at least 100 words.

4 Learn these irregular verbs.

It's a long story
PART 23

INFINITIVE	PAST	PAST PARTICIPLE
ride	rode	ridden
drive	drove	driven (/'drɪvn/)
give	gave	given
draw	drew	drawn
fly	flew	flown

5 Read this with a dictionary.

THE LOCH NESS MONSTER

Loch Ness is an immensely deep lake in the north-eastern Highlands of Scotland. It is overlooked by brooding hills and wild moorland – the perfect setting for strange and unexplained events. In 1933, a motorist on the new lakeside road saw a tremendous upheaval in the loch. The waters churned and boiled as a huge monster, its body the size of a whale, broke the surface. The incident was reported in the local paper, and soon the national press was buzzing with news of what came to be called 'The Loch Ness Monster'. But legends of large water-creatures in Loch Ness go back much further than 1933. In the 6th century AD the Irish missionary Saint Columba was said to have banished a monster which had attacked a swimmer. And local folk tales, going back centuries, speak of 'water horses' and 'water bulls' inhabiting Loch Ness. Scientists have seriously suggested that large creatures may have been stranded in the loch, when 60 million years ago it was cut off from the sea. Perhaps their descendants live there still. But despite hazy photographs, mostly highly magnified, of strange 'humps' in the water, there is very little evidence, as yet, to go on.

(from *Piccolo Explorer Book of Mysteries*)

Parts

 Education

1 Write these fractions in words. Then say them.

³/₇ three sevenths.......... ⁵/₉ .... ¹/₁₀ ....

²/₃ .... ³/₄ .... ³/₁₀ ....

⁴/₅ .... ½ .... ⅛ ....

2 Write a few sentences about the education system in your country.

(When do people start school? When can people leave school? How many pupils finish their education at 18 or later? How many go on to full-time higher education? What examinations are there? How many take them? How many pass?)

3 Read this with a dictionary.

In Britain, the State provides free education up to university level; it is administered by local authorities, but financed partly by the central government. Students have to pay to go to university, but the Ministry of Education and the local authorities give money ('grants') to pay part or all of most students' expenses, including living expenses.

Entrance to university is competitive, but a student can get a place if he or she passes GCE O and A Levels with reasonably good grades. Oxford and Cambridge are no longer reserved for the rich.

Some parents send their children to private schools, either for religious reasons, because of social snobbery, or because they feel these schools will give their children a better education than state schools. A lot of private schools are boarding schools; some of the best-known (e.g. Eton) are traditionally called 'public schools'.

B At the top on the left

1 Say where some of the students usually sit in your classroom. Example:

Jean-Pierre sits at the front on the right; Tomoko
sits at the back between Heinz and Nimet;
Shu Fang sits in the middle of the third row between
Beatrice and Kirsten; Mehrzad sits next to Ewa,
near the back; ...

2 Read this with a dictionary.

In 1979 there were about 220 million people living in the USA. Apart from the American Indians (less than one million), the whole population is descended from immigrants. The greatest proportion are of Anglo-Scottish, Irish, French or Dutch descent, but there are large groups of Italians, Germans, Canadians, Poles, Scandinavians, Russians and Spanish-Americans, and 11% of the population is of African origin. The different groups are not all evenly distributed – for instance in the southern states the population is 52% black. There are more Jews in the USA than in Israel.

3 Try the crossword puzzle.

A C R O S S 6. People who eat with their mouths open .... me.

9. Infinitive of *took*.
10. She gets a lot of ...., but she never takes an aspirin.
12. Don't pick it up by the .... – it's broken.
14. You can read this on some doors.
16. The opposite of *2 down*.
18. 'Where's Susan?' '............ Spain.'
20. Young people in Europe sometimes travel this way.
23. Past of *run*.
25. Are you American .... Canadian?
26. Where are the doors on a bus? At the ....
27. Where is the 12 on a clock? At the ....
29. It's long and yellow.
30. 'Have you finished?' '............ – give me five more minutes.'
31. The opposite of *top*.
33. The opposite of *down*.
35. *Hello* to a friend.
36. Can you .... a bicycle?
39. 'What's the matter with your face?' 'I've got ....'

41. What were the .... of the three fastest cars?
44. I've got a lot of .... in my job; no one ever tells me how to do things.
45. Whisky .... made in Scotland.
46. 'Could I speak to Mary?' '............ can't come to the phone right now, I'm afraid.'
47. She's rather .... at first, but when you get to know her she has got a lot of interesting things to say.
48. 'How did you run in the race?' 'Very ...., I'm afraid.'

DOWN
1. Past of *have*.
2. Where are the red lights on a car? At the ....
3. Don't pull! ....!
4. Past of *come*.
5. .... dear! I *am* sorry.
6. He's been .... since his wife died.
7. 'How .... your son?' 'Fine, thanks.'
8. Seven and three.
11. He's intelligent, but he hasn't had a very good ....
13. Is your cooker .... or gas?
15. The same as *35 across*.
17. She's the fastest woman runner in .... world.
19. ...., I haven't.
21. .... you swim?
22. This chair was made by ....
24. The same as *19 down*.
28. 'Where did you .... my jacket, honey?'
29. 'It's on the table .... the television.'
32. 'What's the ....?' 'I've got toothache.'
34. Just .... the button.
37. I get a letter from him .... ten days or so.
38. 'How long have you been here?' '............ ten minutes.'
40. I'm very .... about the way the government is spending our money.
42. Not different = the ....
43. New York is in the ....
44. Not very many = a ....
47. Nobody was there, ... I came home.

(Solution on page 128.)

C The beginning of the end

1 Turn these sentences into questions.

1. She works on Saturdays. *Does she work on Saturdays?*
2. It's raining. *Is it raining?*
3. My letter arrived. ....
4. Mrs Calloway telephoned this morning. ....

110

5. Your children play tennis. ....

6. Henry was born in England. ....

7. You saw that film on TV last night. ....

....

8. Jane and Susan can swim. ....

9. Dr Croft has got a new car. ....

2 Where does the stress come in these words – at the beginning, in the middle or at the end? And where does /ə/ come?

afraid   better   Britain   breakfast   Switzerland   arrive   England
policeman   question   again   assistant   sentences   secretary   understand

3 Put in suitable words.

1. Education is free, but some people pay to send their children to .... schools.

2. .... children .... school at 16, but .... stay at school until 18.

3. 45 minutes is the same as .... of an hour.

4. Very .... of my friends live in the country; .... of them live in London.

5. .... more pupils pass O Level than A Level.

6. 'Where's the toilet?' 'Up at the .... of the stairs.'

7. I didn't like the film ...., but it got better .... middle.

8. When I go to the cinema I usually sit ...., because I'm short-sighted and I can't see very well.

D What happened next?

1 Correct these sentences.

1. Shakespeare wrote *Don Giovanni*. *Shakespeare didn't write Don Giovanni.*
OR: *Mozart wrote Don Giovanni.*

2. Napoleon studied philosophy in Moscow. ....

....

3. Queen Victoria was married to Louis XIV. ....

....

4. Columbus discovered Australia in 1492. ....

....

5. Charles de Gaulle played football for England. ....

....

111

6. Leonardo da Vinci worked in a restaurant in Rome. ....

....

7. King Herod liked children. ....

8. Oedipus loved his father. ....

9. Mao Tse Tung went from Istanbul to Bombay by bicycle. ....

....

2 What did you do this morning when you woke up?

'First... Then... Next... After that... Finally...'

3 Learn these irregular verbs.

INFINITIVE	PAST	PAST PARTICIPLE
ring	rang	rung
begin	began	begun
stand	stood	stood
understand	understood	understood
sit	sat	sat
lie	lay	lain

4 Read this with a dictionary.

It's a long story PART 24

In her black Porsche, Dr Wagner was getting a little impatient. She was in a hurry to get to her hotel in Inverness and have a bath and a rest, after driving overnight from London. But for the last fifteen miles she had been stuck behind a bus that was driving very slowly in the middle of the road, and it seemed impossible to get past. 'Calm down, Mary,' she said to herself. 'You've got plenty of time.'

   She started thinking about the holiday that was just starting. Every year, she drove up to the Scottish Highlands and spent two weeks looking for the Loch Ness Monster. Dr Wagner was a member of the West London Society for the Investigation of Strange and Unexplained Phenomena, and she was very interested in monsters, ghosts, flying saucers and things of that kind. She had never yet seen anything in Loch Ness, but she always had a wonderful holiday and went back home feeling happy and relaxed. She had a feeling about this year, though. This year was going to be special. Somehow, she just knew.

   A sudden noise brought her out of her dreams. She looked in the mirror. Behind her, the road was full of police cars, with lights flashing and sirens howling. Dr Wagner frowned. She didn't like police cars. 'It's no use making all that noise,' she said. 'You'll never get past the bus.'

Predictions

A Are you sure you'll be all right?

1 What presents do you think people will give you next Christmas, or on your next birthday? Use *I (don't) think*, *I'm sure*, *perhaps*, *probably*. Examples:

I think my father will give me a book
Perhaps somebody will give me perfume.
I don't think anybody will give me a car.

2 If you buy a new car, one day, what will you buy? Why?

3 Read this with a dictionary.

TOMORROW'S WEATHER - CLOUDY WITH LIGHT RAIN

London, SE, Cent S, E England, E Anglia, E Midlands, Channel Islands: Rather cloudy, occasional light rain. Wind W, mainly light. Max temp 12 or 13C (54 or 55F).

W Midlands, SW England, Wales: Cloudy with occasional rain becoming brighter with some showers. Wind W, light or moderate. Max 11 to 12C (52 to 64F).

NW, NE, Cent N England, Lake District, Isle of Man: Cloudy with occasional rain, becoming brighter with some showers. Wind westerly, mainly light. Max 10 or 11C (50 to 52F).

Borders, Edinburgh and Dundee, Aberdeen, Glasgow, SW Scotland, N Ireland: Sunny intervals and showers. Wind westerly light. Max 8 to 10C (46 to 50F).

Cent Highlands, Moray Firth, Argyll, NE, NW Scotland, Orkney, Shetland: Sunny intervals and showers, occasionally heavy and wintry on high ground. Wind westerly, light or moderate. Max 7 to 9C (45 to 48F).

Outlook: Unsettled and windy at times. Temperatures rather below normal.

4 Look again at Unit 9 Lesson C/D. Then write a few sentences to say what the weather will be like tomorrow, in your opinion.

B What will happen next?

1 What will fashions be like in the year 2000? Example:

I think skirts will be *longer* ....

I think the fashionable colour will be ....

I'm sure people will wear ....

I'm sure people won't wear ....

I don't think people will wear ....

People certainly won't wear ....

Perhaps men will wear ....

Perhaps women will wear ....

Clothes will be ....

2 Pronounce these words. (They all have the same vowel sound.)

first   heard   word   early   certain   Thursday   work
shirt   skirt   turn   third   learn   sir   dirty

3 Prepositions. Complete the sentences.

1. Our house is right .... the end of the road.

2. I heard a strange noise .... the middle of the night.

3. My father left school .... 14 and went to work .... a factory.

4. 'How are you going to Paris?' '........... air.'

5. Don't get .... a car before it stops.

6. Don't run until two hours .... eating.

7. Would you like a drink .... you go to bed?

8. Could you take your coat .... my chair, please?

9. I'll meet you at the station, ... the clock.

C What do the stars say?

1 Put in the correct verb form (future with *will* or simple past).

1. My horoscope said 'You *will have* a wonderful week' (have)

2. but actually, I *had* a terrible week. (have)

3. My horoscope said 'You .... on a long journey' (go)

4. but actually, I only .... to the post office. (go)

5. My horoscope said 'Money .... to you' (come)

6. but actually, I .... the whole week paying bills. (spend)

7. My horoscope said 'You .... a tall dark stranger' (meet)

8. but actually, I .... a short fat policeman. (meet)

9. My horoscope said 'This .... a good time for love' (be)

10. but actually, my girlfriend .... very unkind to me. (be)

11. My horoscope said 'There .... bad news on Wednesday'. (be)

12. Actually, there .... bad news every day. (be)

2 Imagine a 'dream holiday' for yourself next year. What will happen? Where will you go? Who will you meet? What will you do?

3 Read this with a dictionary.

(*Which?* is the magazine of the Consumers' Association.
It tests different things that you can buy, and says which is the 'best buy'.
One month, *Which?* tested horoscopes.)

Most people will say there's nothing in horoscopes. So you would expect that most people wouldn't read them. But they do.

We thought we would try to find out how useful forecasts from stars really are, in their most accessible form – horoscopes in the press.

First of all we asked 1,000 people, whether they read horoscopes, whether they found them useful, and what their reactions were.

Their reactions ranged from 'nonsense' and 'a load of rubbish' through 'they're fun' and 'amusing', to one person who always looked at them 'before making any major decision'.

To find out how good the advice and predictions really are, and see if there was any best buy, we asked some 200 people, some men, some women, some believers and some not, to read their horoscopes in the papers and magazines every day for a month, and

to comment on them at the end of each day.

Rather sadly, 83 per cent reported that the advice was very little help at all. There wasn't much to choose between any of the newspapers and magazines we looked at but Woman, Woman's Own and the Daily Mirror were thought marginally less unhelpful than the average, while the Sun and the News of the World were thought worse.

D A matter of life and death

1 Which word or expression is different?

1. top   bottom   front   half   side   back
2. cross   picture   triangle   circle   square
3. beginning   top   middle   end
4. get up   shave   wash   have breakfast
   wake up   go to bed
5. by air   ride   fly   hitchhike   drive

6. racehorse   racing pigeon   lightning
   snail   cheetah
7. best   fastest   very old   most interesting
   worst
8. push   sit down   pick up   pull   turn
9. tomorrow   yesterday   today   Wednesday

2 Put in the correct verb form.

1. Do you often .... John these days? (see)

2. Did you .... the James Bond film on TV yesterday? (see)

3. Have you ever .... an iceberg? (see)

4. I .... your brother in town yesterday. (see)

5. I haven't got Ann's address, but I think my wife .... it. (know)

6. How long have you .... James? (know)

7. For ages – I .... him at school. (know)

8. Can you .... to lunch with us tomorrow? (come)

9. My mother .... to see us every Friday. (come)

10. My parents .... to live in London when I was a baby. (come)

3 Learn these irregular verbs.

INFINITIVE	PAST	PAST PARTICIPLE
build	built	built
send	sent	sent
lend	lent	lent
spend	spent	spent
learn	learnt	learnt

It's a long story PART 25

4 Read this with a dictionary.

Down at the bottom of Loch Ness, things were very calm. The Monster scratched her ear with the third leg on the right and decided that it was time to do something. She didn't usually go up to the surface during the day because the light hurt her eyes, but she was getting bored out of her mind sitting down at the bottom of the loch with nothing to do except talk to the fish. She scratched her ear again, yawned, stretched, and started swimming slowly up towards the light.

Five minutes later, the Monster reached the surface, stuck her head and fifteen metres of neck out of the water, and looked around. She closed her eyes and opened them again. It was a little difficult to understand what was happening. Scotland was generally a fairly quiet place, but today a lot of things seemed to be going on.

On the bank of the loch, two women were fighting. A man was trying to stop them; another man was trying to learn to swim. The road was full of cars with pretty blue lights on top, coming from all directions. A helicopter landed on the bank of the loch and some soldiers got out and lay down. There was a bus driving along very slowly with the driver looking out of the window. The bus driver caught sight of the Monster and drove into the loch. The two women stopped fighting and stood with their mouths open. All the police cars crashed into each other. A sports car stopped and a woman got out and started taking photographs.

It was all too much. The Monster closed her eyes and went back down to the bottom of the loch.

Useful; useless

A All you need is love

1 Write six or more sentences.

> A runner   A photographer
> A skier   An artist   A secretary
> A writer   A businessman
> A teacher   A driver

> needs
>
> does not
> need

> snow.   imagination.
>   a typewriter.   paint.
> money.   patience.   roads.
>   running shoes.   a camera.

2 Put in the correct tense.

1. I *'m going* .... to Lancaster tomorrow. (go)

2. I ...*go*........................... there most weekends. (go)

3. I ...*didn't go*............. there last weekend, though. (not go)

4. 'Where's Alfred?' 'I'm sorry, I ....' (not know)

5. I .... football next Sunday. (play)

6. 'What are you doing?' 'I .... for my shoes.' (look)

7. That child never .... (wash)

8. I .... a great film on TV last night. (see)

9. Everybody looked at Catherine, but nobody .... (speak)

10. 'What did he say?' 'I .... a word.' (not understand)

11. 'Cigar?' 'No, thanks. I ....' (not smoke)

12. I .... born in Hungary. (be)

3 Choose two of these questions and answer them.

What do you need...
1. ...to make a cake?
2. ...to go to China?
3. ...to drive a car?
4. ...to plant a tree?
5. ...to repair a broken tap?
6. ...to make a shirt?

4 Underline the stressed syllables in these
words, like this: calories.
Then circle the vowels that are pronounced /ə/,
like this: calories.
Pronounce the words.

father   family   freedom   water   politicians   important

116

5 Read the text with a dictionary, and answer the questions.

SOME FACTS ABOUT DIET

Your body needs energy, protein, minerals, vitamins and fibre. In order to get all of these it is important to have a varied and balanced diet, and to eat the right amount. Your body 'burns' food to get energy: the amount of energy provided by food is measured in units called calories.

How many calories do you need? This depends on your weight and on what you do. When you are asleep, your body uses nearly one calorie an hour for every kilogram of weight. So a person who weighs seventy kilos uses about 560 calories while sleeping for eight hours; in other words, he needs about 1680 calories just to stay alive for 24 hours, even without doing anything. More calories are needed for different activities – from 100 calories an hour for reading or watching TV, to 350 calories an hour for playing football. To calculate the number of calories needed per day for an average person, first find out that person's ideal weight.

(Your ideal weight is what you *should* weigh. It depends on your height and your build, and it may be very different from your present weight!) Then multiply the correct weight (in kilograms) by 40 for a woman, or 46 for a man. A 57-kilo woman may need about 2300 calories a day – more if she does heavy physical work or a lot of sport, less if she is very inactive.

If you eat more than you need, the extra calories turn into fat; if you eat less than you need, the body burns fat to get energy and you lose weight. One way of losing weight is by dieting – eating less. Another way is to go on eating the same amount, but to increase your body's need for energy by taking more exercise. But be careful. It is important to slim – or to start an exercise programme – gradually. Don't try to lose a lot of weight fast. It doesn't usually work, and it can be dangerous.

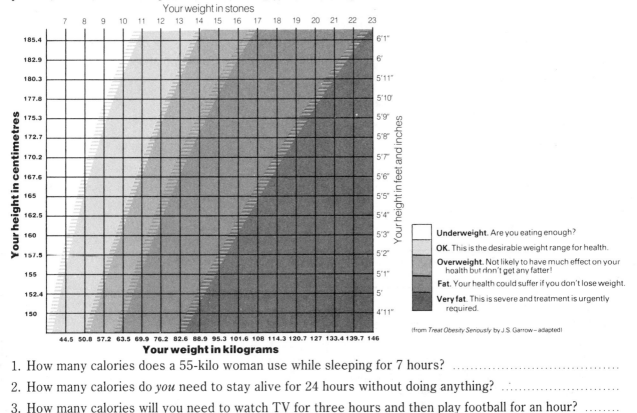

Underweight. Are you eating enough?

OK. This is the desirable weight range for health.

Overweight. Not likely to have much effect on your health but don't get any fatter!

Fat. Your health could suffer if you don't lose weight.

Very fat. This is severe and treatment is urgently required.

(from *Treat Obesity Seriously* by J.S. Garrow – adapted)

1. How many calories does a 55-kilo woman use while sleeping for 7 hours? ....

2. How many calories do *you* need to stay alive for 24 hours without doing anything? ....

3. How many calories will you need to watch TV for three hours and then play football for an hour? ....

4. What is your ideal weight? ....

5. How many calories do you need a day? ....

6. What will happen if an inactive 55-kilo woman eats 2500 calories a day? ....

7. What will happen if an average 70-kilo man eats 2500 calories a day? ....

(Answers on page 128.)

B Is it useful?

1 You take photographs **with a camera.**
How do you:

– eat meat? ....

– cut string? ....

– play a record? ....

– cook food? ....

– find the north? ....

– find out what words mean? ....

– clean your teeth? ....

– wash? ....

2 Imagine you are going to spend six months alone on a small Pacific island. Write a list of ten things that will be useful. Write three things that will be useless. Will anything be necessary?

3 Put in suitable words.

1. Mary .... GCE O .... in maths, English, French, history and art.

2. Winter's coming; it's .... colder.

3. 'What did Paul ....?' 'He said that he .... tired.'

4. Some aeroplanes have a door at the ....

5. I enjoyed the party at the ...., but later it .... very boring.

6. My car's top .... is about 95 ....

7. Please stop that .... – I can't hear anything.

8. 'Where's the lettuce?' 'In the fridge, at the ....'

9. I liked the film, but it had a stupid ....

was	noise	beginning	passed	bottom	back
speed	end	level	got	mph	say	getting

4 Choose one of these three writing exercises.

1. **Complete this story:**
   One evening I was on my way to a party with my brother Phil.
   Suddenly the car stopped. There was no petrol!
2. **Write a story containing these objects:**
   a thermometer, a banana, a telephone, a chair, a watch.
3. **Write a true or imagined story about not having something you needed.**

Useful words: then	after that	so	and	but
and then	finally			

C It's useless (part one)

1 Complete the conversations.

A: Can I .... you?

B: Yes, I .... some furniture.

A: .... floor, sir.

———◇———

A: .... speak to you .... minutes?

B: Well, I'm afraid .... busy. Can you wait .... tomorrow?

———◇———

A: .... manager?

B: No, sir, I'm not.

A: Well, I .... to .... the manager.

B: Have you ....?

A: No. I ....

2 Countable or uncountable?

COUNTABLE	UNCOUNTABLE	COUNTABLE	UNCOUNTABLE
floor	water	....	....
shop	wool	....	....
car	cheese	....	....
complaint	hair	....	....
		....	....
		....	....

furniture	coffee
bicycle	food
headache	watch
money	letter
rain	weather
bottle	pen

3 Say these sentences with the right stress.

1. It's a *beautiful* day.
2. I don't want *three* tickets, I want *four* tickets.
3. Not *furniture* – the *manager*.
4. I *am* sorry.
5. I said *Tuesday*, not *Thursday*.

4 You are going to exchange letters with a British or American pen-friend called Martin Croft. Write your first letter, in which you introduce yourself and say something about your life, work and interests.

D It's useless (part two)

1 You can buy **shoes** at a **shoe shop**. Where can you buy:

records.. antiques..

paint .... furniture ....

wine ....

119

Find out from your dictionary what you can buy at:

a butcher's ....

an ironmonger's ....

a grocer's ....

a greengrocer's ....

a stationer's ....

a baker's ....

a dairy ....

2 **Read this letter and put in suitable words.**

14 Hillcrest Drive
Pemberton
Lancashire

The ....
Northern Gas Showrooms
87 High Street
Cokerborough
Lancashire

14 July, 1982

Dear Sir,

I am writing to .... about a cooker which I ....
from you in June. ....of all, it was delivered very late:
I ordered the cooker in the first week of June, and it ....
not arrive...........10 July.

..........ly, the cooker does not............. ....I turn it
on, very little gas comes out..........the burners. It is
impossible to cook anything because the cooker does not get
..........enough.

..........ly, you have sent me a............for £14.50 for
'installation'. When I bought the..........., you told me that
the..........included installation.

I look forward to hearing ....you,

..........faithfully,

Angela B Pettigrew

Angela B. Pettigrew

3 **Write a letter to:**
Foster & Bradley Ltd
38 The Broadway
Bridgnorth
Shropshire WV16 3HT
Great Britain

about one of these things which arrived late, didn't work, etc.:
– a tape recorder
– a calculator
– a camera

4 **Learn these irregular verbs.**

INFINITIVE	PAST	PAST PARTICIPLE
lose	lost	lost
fight	fought	fought
fall	fell	fallen
rise	rose	risen
forget	forgot	forgotten

5 Read this with a dictionary.

'Hello, Judy,' said Dr Wagner. 'What are you doing here? I thought you were in Rio.' 'It's a long story,' said Judy. 'I'll tell you later.' 'Did you see the Monster?' said Dr Wagner. 'Wasn't she just *wonderful*? I got hundreds of photos.'

'I'm sorry to interrupt,' said Jasper, 'but I think this is a very good time to go on holiday. Isabel, go and get Sam out of the water and follow us up to the castle. Judy, come with me. I hope the ghost remembered to fill the plane up with petrol.' 'Ghost?' said Dr Wagner. 'You have a ghost in your castle? A *ghost*?' 'Come along with us and you can meet him,' said Judy. 'But hurry.'

Twenty seconds later, they drove in through the front gate of the castle in Dr Wagner's Porsche, and a minute or so after that Isabel ran up carrying Sam over her shoulder. The ghost closed the gate and led the way to the back of the castle. There, standing on the grass, shining in the sun, was a powerful-looking six-seater aeroplane. 'Get in,' said Jasper. 'We haven't got

a moment to lose.' 'Can I come too?' asked Dr Wagner. 'I must talk to that beautiful ghost.' 'Of course,' said Jasper, 'but get in fast, or you'll be talking to our wonderful police. Fasten seat-belts, everybody. Take-off in fifteen seconds.' 'Where are we going?' asked Judy. 'Rio,' said Jasper. 'That's where you wanted to go, isn't it?' 'Sounds good to me,' said Sam. 'Jasper,' said Judy, 'I have been a blind, blind fool. I love you.'

Self and others

A Do it yourself

1 Six people from different countries are in the same compartment on a long train journey. They would like to talk to each other. The table shows the languages that they speak.

	English	French	Chinese	Japanese	Spanish	German	Swahili	Arabic	Russian
Alicia		✓			✓				
Shu Fang			✓		✓				
John	✓						✓	✓	
Yasuko	✓		✓	✓					
Mohammed Ali						✓		✓	
Erika	✓	✓				✓			✓

Write sentences to say how different people can talk to each other. Examples:

Alicia and Shu Fang can talk to each other in Spanish.
Alicia and Yasuko can talk to each other if Shu Fang interprets for them.

2 Do you do these things yourself, or does somebody else do them for you? Examples:

I repair my car myself.
Somebody else washes my clothes.

1. repair your car/bicycle/motorbike

2. wash your clothes

3. clean your house/flat/room

4. answer your letters

5. make your bed

6. iron your clothes

7. buy your food

8. cook your food

3 Read this with a dictionary.

WHAT A BLESSING YOUNGER BROTHERS ARE

When my sister says to me,
'Go and put the kettle on,'
I say to my younger brother,
'Go and put the kettle on,'
So my brother goes and puts the kettle on.
When my younger brother says to me,
'Bring a tin of fruit up,'
I say to my elder sister,
'Bring a tin of fruit up,'
But she says,
'Go yourself you lazy thing,'
So I say to my younger brother,
'Go yourself you lazy thing!'
So he goes and brings the tin of fruit up.

Catherine Frankland (aged 13)

"I just shook his hand and he was sick."

4 These texts were written by children. Read them with a dictionary. (Note: 'newsance' = *nuisance* – something irritating.)

You have to love your own baby because everyone else finds them a newsance.

Patrick aged 8

I know my mother and Father Love each other because my mother cooks him his favorite roast every night

Theresa aged 8

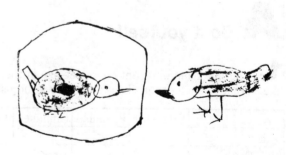

My budgie broke is neck because he was always kissing himsel in the mirrer.

Tim aged

love is important becaus if people did not love each other there wouldn't be any people.

Lynn aged 7

122

B Shall I open it for you?

1 Complete the dialogues.

POLLY: Hello, Sue. Been shopping?

SUE: Hello, Polly. Yes. It's terrible. Millions of people in the ....

POLLY: .... carry something .... you?

SUE: Oh, that's .... of you. Thanks. How are you?

POLLY: Fine, thanks. Thirsty. .... a cup of tea? My flat's just round the corner.

SUE: Not just ...., thanks. I have to be home before five. But come and have tea at my place.

POLLY: Thank you .... I'd ....

—◇—

SUE: Come in, Polly. Put the shopping .... the table. .... your coat?

POLLY: No, thanks. I'll keep .... I'm very .... today.

SUE: Tea .... coffee?

POLLY: I'd prefer coffee, if ....

SUE: Yes, ... course. And .... toast?

POLLY: Yes, I'd .... Can I do anything?

SUE: No, just sit down and get warm. I'll put some music on, ... I?

POLLY: That .... nice.

2 Put in *me, you, him, her* etc.; *myself, yourself, himself, herself* etc.; *each other; somebody else.*

1. 'Mary's going to marry a Japanese.' 'Good heavens! How will they understand ....?'

2. I often talk to .... when I'm alone.

3. 'I don't like these flowers.' 'Well, give them to ....' 'Who?' '......................'

4. 'Why are you walking like that?' 'I hurt .... when I was playing football.'

5. 'Who went with ....?' 'Nobody. She went by ....'

6. Stop looking at ....in the mirror; you're not as beautiful as all that.

7. 'Who does the cleaning for old Mrs Collins?' 'Nobody. She does it ....'

8. Little Alice is only two, but she can dress ....

9. He never listens to ...., and she never listens to ....

3 Put in *at, to, with, about, for,* or *by.*

1. They can only talk .... each other if somebody interprets.

2. They're always talking .... politics.

3. 'Can I help you?' 'No, thanks – I can do it .... myself.'

4. In England we only shake hands .... people if we haven't seen them for a long time.

5. Look .... this photo of Harry. He looks just like his father.

6. 'What's that?' 'A bottle of perfume .... my mother.'

7. Stop thinking .... work and listen .... me. I want to talk .... you.

123

4 Put in *'ll, shall, would, 'd* or *could.*

1. I .... answer the door, shall I?

2. .... you like a drink?

3. That .... be nice.

4. I .... prefer orange juice.

5. .... I take your coat?

6. I .... like a single to Manchester, please.

7. .... I have some more potatoes, please?

8. How much sugar .... you like in your tea?

9. Excuse me. .... you possibly tell me the way to the station?

10. .... I open the door for you?

11. 'I'm going to hitchhike to Scotland.'
   'You .... get lost.'

C Whose is that?

1 Write and pronounce the contractions.

do not *don't* I have .... I will .... she is .... she has .... they are ....

we are .... they will .... will not .... cannot .... is not .... I am ....

does not .... could not .... you are .... was not .... has not .... I would ....

2 Are you a good detective?

The police stop a car. There are three people in the car: John, Ann and Mary. On the back seat there is a pistol.
John says: 'It's mine'. Ann says: 'It's hers'. Mary says: 'It's his'.
Nobody is telling the truth. Whose is the pistol?

3 More detection.

In the car, the police find a diamond necklace, a valuable painting and a fur coat. The police find out that they belong to a film star, a businessman and a doctor. The diamonds don't belong to the doctor. The coat doesn't belong to the businessman. The painting belongs to a woman. The film star never wears fur coats. Who does the painting belong to?

(Solutions on page 128.)

4 Try this crossword puzzle.

ACROSS

1. These are useful when it's sunny.
6. I never go to the hairdresser's – I've always cut my hair ....
9. I'm afraid I have got a .... My toaster still doesn't work.
10. Where .... Volvo cars made?
11. Not difficult.
12. John .... his back carrying books yesterday. He's not going to play football today.
14. Could you switch the light ...., please?
15. Please .... down. I'll be with you in a minute.
16. Did you and the Cooks come in your car or ....?
17. 'Is this yours or Jane's?' 'It's ...., I think.'
18. Can be made of cotton, useful for camping. (plural)
20. This doesn't really .... to me – I've just borrowed it for the weekend.

124

23. Singular of *18 across*.
24. They've travelled all .... China since they've been there.
27. Who .... the Nobel prize for literature this year?
29. I've .... a baby since I last saw you.
30. 'Oh, dear! I haven't got a pen.' 'Would you like to borrow ....?'
31. I quite like white wine, but I .... red wine.
32. A very small .... is easier to travel with than a one-year-old.
33. Did you go to Japan for your holiday again this year or did you go somewhere ....?
34. Who's going to .... your boss when he goes to Hong Kong?

D
O
W
N

1. When you meet someone for the first time, you usually .... hands.
2. Biology is .... if you want to be a doctor.
3. I've got an .... with the dentist next Thursday at 10.15.

4. .... I switch the light on for you?
5. I've got two daughters and a ....
7. My family's fine, thanks – and ....?
8. Can you buy .... fish at your local supermarket?
12. Are you sure this is yours? John said it was ....
13. Were the tomatoes fresh or ....?
17. A student .... is cheaper than a hotel.
19. I don't want to go there. First of all, it's a long way. And ...., I'm tired.
21. We borrowed my sister's car last week when .... was in the garage.
22. That's .... – I thought I had £5 in my wallet, but there's only £1 here now.
25. Knowing French is .... if you're learning Italian.
26. You open this to get into a house.
28. What time did you wake .... this morning?
32. Can you .... here at 7.15?

(Solution on page 128.)

D Do you ever talk to yourself?

1 Put in *anybody, anything, anywhere, somebody, something, somewhere, everybody, everything, everywhere, nobody, nothing* or *nowhere*.

1. 'Mary's at the door.' 'I don't want to see ....'
2. They're a very loving couple. They go .... together.
3. I can't find my glasses. I know they're .... in this room.
4. Let me give you .... to eat.
5. 'Do you know Sid?' 'Yes, ... knows Sid.'
6. 'Is .... all right?' 'Yes, thanks.'
7. I need .... to love me.
8. I can't find my glasses ....
9. 'Did .... telephone yesterday?' 'No, ...'
10. I can't understand .... that she says.
11. 'What would you like?' '.................. just now, thank you.'
12. 'Where can we sit?' '.................., I'm afraid. It's full.'

2 Learn these irregular verbs.

INFINITIVE	PAST	PAST PARTICIPLE
teach	taught	taught
keep	kept	kept
shut	shut	shut

3 Past participles. Put the correct verb form in each blank. The infinitives are given below.

1. Have you .... your children to the new swimming pool?

2. It was a terrible accident – his leg was .... in three places.

3. I *am* sorry, but I've .... your surname.

4. Has he .... your parents yet?

5. I've .... this watch since I was six.

6. Are you alone, or has John .... too?

7. It's a British car, but some of the parts were .... in Spain.

8. It's so nice and quiet here – I haven't .... so well since I was a child!

9. Have you .... this morning's newspaper?

10. Not much was .... about how the continents were formed until 25 years ago.

11. Has she ever .... on the left side of the road before?

12. When I was in school, we were .... by a bell ringing at 6.30.

13. That young boy that was missing was .... dead in a pond this morning.

14. Since this stamp was .... on my passport, I've never .... any trouble getting in or out of England.

15. I don't know when he started working here, but he's .... here for a long time.

16. Do you know how much money is .... on medicine in England every year?

17. Is English .... in primary school in your country?

18. I've .... most of the others, but Jean doesn't know yet.

19. It's .... very difficult to get a good connection on our phone.

20. Have you .... everything you need for dinner, or would you like me to pick something up on my way home?

be	become	break	buy	come	drive
find	forget	have (twice)		know	make
meet	put	read	sleep	spend	take
teach	tell	wake up			

4 Read this with a dictionary.

As the plane flew peacefully south-west across the Atlantic, Judy put her head on Jasper's shoulder and closed her eyes. 'I'm so glad I'm in love with you instead of Sam,' she said. 'It's much nicer. I'm sure we're going to be very happy together. Do you think the others will be all right?' 'I think so,' said Jasper, and kissed her.

Judy listened to the fragments of conversation that came from the seats behind. 'Isabel, you are my favourite detective. Will you teach me to swim?' 'Have some more champagne, ghost.' 'Yes, please. Call me MacDonald.' 'You've got beautiful eyes, Sam.' 'Can ghosts get married?'

'Sounds all right,' said Judy. 'Tell me, are you really terribly rich? How did you get your money? What do you do, actually? How did you get to know Sam? Why did you really hijack that plane?'

'I'll tell you later,' said Jasper. 'It's a long story.'

THERE IS NO PRACTICE BOOK WORK FOR UNIT 32.

Solutions

Unit 1, Lesson B

4

Unit 3, Lesson D

1

Unit 5, Lesson D

1

Unit 6, Lesson A

3 Catherine.

Unit 7, Lesson D

4 There are 29 different triangles.

Unit 8, Lesson A

3 1. True (between Alaska and Siberia)
  2. False (but in 1610 it was true)
  3. False (15 million in 1980)
  4. False (4807 metres)
  5. False (100)
  6. True
  7. False (it's in Scotland)
  8. False (1.6)
  9. True
  10. False (in the Antarctic)

Unit 9, Lesson A

4

Unit 9, Lesson B

1 1. Crocodiles live in rivers.
  2. Snakes can't dance.
  3. There are no snakes in Ireland.
  4. Australians speak English.
  5. Austrians speak German.
  6. No. A marathon is just over 42km long.
  7. There are no elephants in Brazil.
  8. Washington is the capital of the USA.
  9. Buenos Aires is the capital of Argentina.
  10. The Pope speaks English (and several other languages).
  11. Shakespeare was English.
  12. The Kama Sutra is a book about love.

Unit 13, Lesson A

4

Unit 14, Lesson B

4 Valerie is not the organist, so put *no* in that column.
Lorna cannot speak German, so put *no* in that column.
Mary cannot speak Italian, so put *no* in that column.
Anthea cannot play the violin, so put *no* in that column.
Anthea cannot speak Spanish, so put *no* in that column.
Valerie can't speak French, so put *no* in that column.
Lorna doesn't play the harp, so put *no* in that column.
The girl who plays the violin speaks French, so
  Valerie (who doesn't speak French) cannot play the violin.
  Put a *no* in that column.
This puts three *no*s in the violin column; so Lorna
  is the one who can play the violin, and since the
  girl who plays the violin speaks French, that is
  Lorna, too. Put *yes* in those two columns and *no* in all
  Lorna's other columns.
This puts three *no*s in the organ column. Put *yes* in
  Anthea's organ column and *no* in her other
  instrument columns.
The organist can't speak Italian, so put *no*
  in Anthea's Italian column.
This leaves Valerie who can speak Italian; put *yes*
  there and *no* in the other language columns.
This means Mary can speak Spanish, which means
  Anthea can speak German.
The only harp column now free is Valerie's.
  Valerie can speak Italian and play the harp.

Unit 15, Lesson D

1

Unit 21, Lesson D

2

Unit 28, Lesson B

3

Unit 17, Lesson B

4

Unit 23, Lesson B

4

Unit 30, Lesson A

5
1. 55 calories an hour × 7 hours = 385 calories
2. Your weight in kilos × 24
3. 100 × 3 + 350 = 650 calories
4. Look at the chart.
5. Your ideal weight (in kilos) × 40 if you are a woman; your ideal weight (in kilos) × 46 if you are a man; (more if you are very active, less if you are inactive).
6. 55 × 40 = 2200 calories a day needed. So the extra calories wi turn into fat.
7. 70 × 46 = 3220 calories a day needed. So the body will burn fat to get energy and he will lose weight.

Unit 19, Lesson A

1 O'Connor is singing folk songs.
Ducarme is acting in *Hamlet*.
Haas is lecturing on butterflies.
Carlotti is playing the violin.

Unit 19, Lesson B

4

Unit 25, Lesson C

4

Unit 27, Lesson B

2 Alice talks fastest.

Unit 31, Lesson C

2 The pistol is Ann's.

3 The painting belongs to the film star.

4

Unit 20, Lesson C

4
1. Washington
2. Belfast
3. Twelve
4. European Economic Community
5. Yes
6. In Egypt
7. India, south-east Asia, Africa.
8. Volkswagen, Mercedes, Audi, Opel, Porsche, BMW, . . .
9. Eight
10. St Petersburg/Petrograd
11. It's very unusual – polar bears live in the Arctic and penguins live in the Antarctic.
12. Twenty-five

WITHDRAWN